Building Your Linux Server Mastery:

A Complete Guide to Linux Structure & Commands

Written by, Lynne Kolestar

Introduction

Welcome to the ultimate guide for mastering Linux! This comprehensive book is designed to serve as an easy-to-find, easy-to-read reference for Linux's structure and commands. With clear text and a well-organized layout, it's ideal for quick lookups as well as more in-depth exploration of Linux essentials.

What sets this book apart is its added value — concise, user-friendly explanations that provide just enough detail to refresh your memory on the function of each command. Think of it as your personal, enhanced version of the Linux manpages, offering quick answers without needing to go online, and with greater clarity and convenience. Whether you're a seasoned pro or just starting out, this guide will quickly become an invaluable tool in your Linux toolkit.

Table of Contents

Chapter 1: Navigating the Linux Filesystem

Filesystem Hierarchy: Full reference to key directories

A complete list of typical Linux directories found in a standard filesystem, along with their purposes, historical context, and common usage:

/ (Root Directory) & /root Directory

/ (Root Directory)
The top-level directory containing the entire Linux filesystem.

/root - The home directory for the root user (the superuser with highest privileges), kept separate from /home for security and clarity.

Separation for Security: Keeping /root distinct reduces the risk of accidental damage to critical files and isolates root's environment during system issues.
Critical Role in System Recovery: Since /root is within the root filesystem, it remains accessible even if /home is on a separate, unmounted partition.

Permissions: Accessible only by the root user, ensuring the security of sensitive administrative files.

/bin – Essential user command binaries

The /bin directory contains essential system binaries (executables) required for basic system operations and maintenance.

Purpose: Contains essential user command binaries (executables) required for basic system functionality, available even in single-user mode.

Key Commands in /bin:

ls (list contents)

cp (copy files)

mv (move files)

rm (remove files)

cat (concatenate files)

bash (default shell)

System Recovery: Provides critical tools for troubleshooting, mounting filesystems, and managing files during recovery or emergency modes.

Accessible to All Users: Tools in /bin are available to all users, not just root, for basic operations.

Part of Root Filesystem: Resides in the root filesystem, ensuring it's available even when other filesystems aren't mounted.

Historical Context: /bin was originally for essential binaries, while /usr/bin held non-essential tools. Some modern distributions have merged /bin with /usr/bin, with /bin often linking to /usr/bin for compatibility.

/sbin - System binaries for administrators

The /sbin directory contains system binaries essential for system administration tasks and maintenance, typically used by the root user.

Purpose: Contains system binaries for administrative tasks, primarily used by the root user (system administrator) for maintenance and configuration.

Key Commands in /sbin:

ifconfig or ip (network configuration)

fdisk (disk partitioning)

reboot (restart system)

mount (mount filesystems)

fsck (filesystem check)

Restricted to Administrators: Commands are generally for the root user or users with elevated privileges, often requiring sudo for execution.

System Boot and Recovery: Essential during boot and recovery for tasks like initializing hardware, mounting filesystems, and system repairs.

Part of Root Filesystem: Resides in the root filesystem to ensure availability even when other filesystems (like /usr) are not mounted.

Historical Context: Created to separate user commands (/bin) from administrative commands (/sbin) for better organization.

Relationship with /usr/sbin: /usr/sbin holds additional admin tools not critical for system startup, unlike /sbin.

Modern Usage: On some systems, /sbin may be merged with /usr/sbin, often as a symbolic link, but its core function remains the same.

/etc - Configuration files for system
The /etc directory contains system configuration files that control system settings and behavior.

Purpose: Stores host-specific configuration files that control system behavior and services.

Key Files in /etc:

/etc/passwd: User account details.

/etc/fstab: Filesystem mount points.

/etc/ssh/: SSH service configuration.

/etc/network/interfaces or **/etc/netplan/:** Network settings.

System Customization: Used to configure OS components, services (e.g., web servers), and security policies (e.g., firewall, authentication).

Static Data: Contains only static configuration files—no binaries or runtime data.

Organization: Files are service-specific (e.g., /etc/nginx/nginx.conf for Nginx) and grouped in subdirectories (e.g., /etc/systemd/).

Historical Context: Originally "etcetera," now standardized for system configurations.

Critical in Boot Process: Files like /etc/inittab and /etc/rc.local help initialize services and hardware during boot.

Consistency Across Distributions: All Linux distributions use /etc for configuration, providing uniformity for administrators.

Writable by Root: Root user can modify configurations; regular users typically have read-only access.

/usr - User binaries and system resources
The /usr directory contains user applications, libraries, and shared resources for system-wide use.

Purpose: Stores non-essential user applications, libraries, documentation, and resources.

Key Subdirectories:

/usr/bin: User-level applications (e.g., grep, vim).

/usr/sbin: Administrative tools not required for boot (e.g., apache2, iptables).

/usr/lib: Shared libraries for applications.

/usr/share: Architecture-independent data (e.g., man pages, icons).

/usr/local: Locally installed or custom software.

Separation from Core Software: Unlike core files in /bin and /sbin, /usr contains optional software and add-ons.

Centralized Resource Management: Stores executables, libraries, manuals, headers, and source files.

Multi-User Support: Provides tools and applications available to all users after system boot.

Historical Context: Originally for user home directories, now used for applications and system tools.

FHS Compliance: /usr is shareable, often mounted separately, and should be read-only.

Modern Usage: Many Linux systems merge /bin, /sbin, and /lib into /usr/bin, /usr/sbin, and /usr/lib for simplicity.

/var - Variable data and logs storage

Variable data files that change dynamically, including logs (/var/log), mail spools, temporary files, and databases.

Purpose: Stores variable data files that change dynamically, including logs, mail spools, temporary files, and databases.

Key Subdirectories in /var:

/var/log: Contains system logs, such as error messages and event tracking.

/var/spool: Holds data for queued tasks like print jobs, mail, or cron jobs.

/var/tmp: Stores temporary files that persist across reboots.

/var/lib: Contains application-specific data, including database files.

/var/cache: Caches application data, such as downloaded software packages or web browser cache.

System Operation:

Dynamic Data: /var stores data that frequently changes during system operation, helping separate static files from dynamic ones.

Logging: Essential for system administration, with logs found in /var/log for troubleshooting.

Task Spooling: /var/spool manages queued tasks (e.g., print jobs, emails) for orderly processing.

Temporary File Storage: /var/tmp holds files that need to persist across reboots, used by applications during runtime.

Historical Context: Initially created to separate dynamic data from static files in Unix systems, ensuring efficient system management.
Filesystem Hierarchy: According to the Filesystem Hierarchy Standard (FHS), /var holds data that can grow over time and may need to be mounted on its own partition for large-scale systems.

Writable by Root: As /var contains dynamic data, it is typically writable by the root user, with regular users often having limited access.

/tmp Temporary files and data storage

The /tmp directory stores temporary files created by applications and the system.

Purpose: Stores temporary files created by applications or the system during runtime. Files in /tmp are typically cleared on reboot and are not intended to persist after they are no longer needed.

Key Characteristics of /tmp:

Temporary Data Storage: /tmp is used by applications and the operating system to store data that is only required for a short period of time, such as session files or intermediary data. Once the program completes or the system reboots, these files are deleted.

Shared Usage: /tmp is accessible by all processes running on the system. Applications can write to /tmp without needing to know about each other's temporary data.

System-Wide Access: Unlike user-specific directories like /home, /tmp is world-writable, allowing any user or process to store data there.

Common Use Cases for /tmp:

Session Files: Temporary files that are used by applications for the duration of a session (e.g., a text editor saving unsaved work).

Interim Files: Files generated during processing that are required temporarily (e.g., a compression tool creating a temporary file before moving the final output).

Lock Files: Used to prevent multiple instances of an application from running simultaneously and causing conflicts.

Web Servers and Databases: Temporary session data or cached queries are often stored in /tmp.

Role of /tmp in System Operation:

Efficient Data Handling: By isolating temporary files, /tmp prevents unnecessary clutter in other directories, ensuring that important data is not mixed with transient information.

Improved Security: The contents of /tmp are regularly cleaned up, either automatically or on reboot, to reduce the risk of accumulated or potentially malicious files.

System Performance: Many systems configure /tmp as a tmpfs (temporary filesystem), meaning it resides in RAM for faster access and to reduce wear on disk-based storage.

Historical Background: /tmp has been a part of Unix systems since the beginning, initially used to store temporary files in various locations. Its creation helped standardize the process by providing a single, designated space for temporary data.

Relationship with System Hierarchy:

Part of the Filesystem Hierarchy Standard (FHS): According to the FHS, /tmp is a designated directory for temporary files, and its contents are considered ephemeral.

Cleanup Requirements: The FHS specifies that the contents of /tmp may be deleted at any time, especially after a reboot.

Security Considerations:

World-Writable by Default: Since /tmp is world-writable, any user or process can write to it. This presents potential security risks, as malicious software could exploit this access. To mitigate this, some distributions enforce stricter permissions or use the noexec option to prevent the execution of scripts in /tmp.

Automatic Cleanup: Many systems clean up /tmp either periodically or during a reboot to ensure it does not become filled with unused files.

Modern Usage of /tmp:
On modern Linux systems, /tmp is typically configured to use tmpfs, a temporary filesystem stored in RAM, which speeds up access to temporary files and reduces wear on physical storage.

Temporary Storage: As part of the FHS, /tmp is designed for data that should not persist and can be safely discarded once no longer needed.

Summary: /tmp is a critical directory for storing temporary files created during system and application execution. It provides a shared space for transient data, improving system organization, security, and performance. By following the Filesystem Hierarchy Standard, /tmp ensures that temporary files are handled efficiently, with provisions for automatic cleanup and optimized storage using tmpfs.

/home - User personal files and directories

The /home directory stores individual user directories, providing isolated space for personal files, configurations, and data in multi-user environments.

Purpose of /home: The /home directory is intended for storing user-specific data, including documents, configurations, applications, and personal files. It separates user data from system files, making it easier to manage, back up, and transfer.

Key Characteristics of /home

User Data Storage: The main function of /home is to store personal files. Each user has their own subdirectory (e.g., /home/username).

Personal Configuration Files: /home contains user-specific settings, often stored in hidden files (e.g., .bashrc, .vimrc).

Separation of User and System Files: Unlike system directories (e.g., /bin, /etc), /home isolates user data, ensuring it doesn't interfere with critical system files.

Common Use Cases for /home

User Files: Documents, images, videos, and other personal data are stored in a user's home directory.

Example: /home/username/Documents, /home/username/Pictures

User Configuration: Applications store configuration files here, enabling users to retain preferences across sessions.

Example: .bashrc, .vimrc, .config/

Application Data: Some applications store user-specific data, such as saved games or application-generated files.

Example: /home/username/.mozilla (for Firefox data), /home/username/.steam (for Steam game data)

Personal Scripts and Binaries: Users can store their custom scripts or locally compiled binaries here.
Example: /home/username/scripts, /home/username/bin

Role of /home in System Operation

User Isolation: /home isolates each user's personal data, which is crucial in multi-user systems where data privacy and integrity are important.

Data Persistence: Unlike temporary directories like /tmp, files in /home are intended for long-term storage and persist across system reboots.

Backup and Migration: As /home contains valuable user data, it's often the primary target for backup operations.

Historical Background

Originally, Unix systems stored user directories within the /usr directory. As systems grew, it became necessary to isolate user data into its own directory, leading to the introduction of /home to centralize and organize user data separately from system files.

Relationship with System Hierarchy

The /home directory follows the Filesystem Hierarchy Standard (FHS), which specifies that:
/home is dedicated to user directories.
Each user gets their own subdirectory, named after their username, where personal files and configurations are stored.

Security Considerations

File Permissions: Each user has control over their subdirectory, ensuring they cannot modify others' data. The system administrator (root) can manage all directories, but users can't alter data outside their home directory.

User Privacy: File permissions prevent unauthorized access to other users' files, ensuring privacy. By default, users should not be able to access each other's directories unless explicitly allowed.

Modern Usage of /home

On modern Linux systems, /home continues to serve as the primary location for user data. It may be mounted on its own partition or disk, offering several benefits. Additionally, /home is often used in hosting environments, where the public_html directory inside each user's home directory serves as web space for hosting personal or private websites.

Separation of User Data: Isolating /home helps preserve user data even during system reinstallation or upgrades.

Backup Flexibility: With /home on a separate partition, user data can be backed up independently of the rest of the system.

/home Partition

In some configurations, /home is mounted as a separate partition, distinct from the root filesystem. This configuration offers several advantages:

Isolation of User Data: /home can be managed independently of system files, simplifying upgrades or reinstalls.

Backup Ease: A separate /home partition allows for easy, independent backups of user data.

User Customization

The /home directory provides a space for users to fully customize their environment. Users can modify configuration files, store custom scripts, and install personal applications without requiring administrator privileges.

Part of the Filesystem Hierarchy Standard (FHS)

User Data Location: /home is designated for storing user-specific data and settings, separate from system files.

Default User Directory: Each user has a directory under /home named after their username (e.g., /home/alice, /home/bob).

Summary

The /home directory is crucial for organizing user-specific files and configurations. It ensures user data is separate from system files, allows users to customize their environment, and simplifies backup and migration. As part of the Filesystem Hierarchy Standard, it provides a consistent, accessible location for personal data, offering both privacy and flexibility for users and administrators.

/lib - Essential system libraries and modules

The /lib directory stores essential shared libraries and kernel modules required for the system to boot and run applications.

Purpose of /lib

Shared Libraries: /lib holds essential libraries required for the system's basic functionality. These libraries provide common routines and services used by various programs, helping them interact with the operating system without having to include these functions within their own code.

Kernel Modules: /lib/modules contains kernel modules that extend the capabilities of the Linux kernel. These modules are dynamically loaded as needed to support various hardware devices or additional features (e.g., new file systems, networking protocols).

Key Characteristics of /lib

Essential Libraries: These libraries are crucial for core system operations, providing functions that manage memory, perform input/output operations, and make system calls.

Example:
/lib/libc.so (C standard library), /lib/libm.so (math library)

Shared Object Files: Many programs rely on shared libraries (also known as .so files) for execution. These libraries contain reusable code that different programs can call, reducing redundancy.

Example: /lib/x86_64-linux-gnu/libc.so.6

Kernel Modules: /lib/modules stores kernel modules, which allow the kernel to support a variety of hardware devices and functionalities. These modules can be loaded into the kernel without rebooting the system.

Example:
/lib/modules/5.4.0-74-
generic/kernel/drivers/net/ethernet/realtek/r8169.ko

Role of /lib in System Operation

Basic System Operations: Libraries in /lib provide the necessary functionality for fundamental system operations, such as the C library (libc), which is relied upon by many user programs.

Program Execution: When a program is executed, the system loads the required libraries from /lib into memory, enabling the program to use system resources efficiently.

Device and Hardware Support: Kernel modules stored in /lib/modules extend the kernel's functionality to support a range of hardware and devices (e.g., network cards, printers).

Historical Background
In early Unix systems, shared libraries were introduced to avoid redundant code across applications. Over time, the /lib directory evolved to hold both essential shared libraries and kernel modules, centralizing these critical components needed for system operation.

Relationship with the System Hierarchy
According to the Filesystem Hierarchy Standard (FHS), the /lib directory should store libraries essential for system boot and running core system binaries found in /bin or /sbin. Non-essential libraries are typically stored in /usr/lib.

Essential Libraries: Libraries required for system booting and core applications.

Optional Libraries: Libraries not critical to system booting, stored in /usr/lib or /usr/local/lib.

Security Considerations

File Permissions: Only system administrators (root) can modify files in /lib, ensuring the integrity of system libraries and preventing unauthorized changes.

Read-Only for Users: Regular users cannot alter the files in /lib, ensuring that essential libraries remain intact and preventing accidental system instability.

Modern Usage of /lib
In modern Linux distributions:
Separation of Libraries by Architecture: On multi-architecture systems, /lib may contain directories for each architecture (e.g., /lib/x86_64-linux-gnu for 64-bit systems).

Library Linking: Applications in /bin or /sbin rely on libraries in /lib to function, with the system loading these libraries as needed.

/lib and /usr/lib

Core vs. Non-Essential Libraries: /lib contains critical libraries, while /usr/lib holds non-essential libraries, supporting user applications that aren't needed for system boot. This separation ensures that critical libraries are available immediately during boot.

User Applications: Libraries in /usr/lib support programs in /usr/bin and /usr/sbin, but they are not essential for booting the system.

Kernel Modules

/lib/modules holds kernel modules that can be loaded dynamically to extend the functionality of the Linux kernel. These modules are stored in version-specific directories, ensuring compatibility with the current kernel.

Example: /lib/modules/5.4.0-74-generic/

Summary

The /lib directory is crucial for the basic operation of a Linux system, as it stores shared libraries necessary for running system binaries and applications, along with kernel modules that extend the kernel's functionality. These files are vital for maintaining system stability and efficiency, and as outlined by the Filesystem Hierarchy Standard (FHS), /lib is dedicated to system-critical components, ensuring the system can boot, execute essential programs, and interface with hardware devices.

/opt - Optional application software packages

The /opt directory stores optional, self-contained software packages, often third-party applications, that are not part of the core operating system.

Purpose of /opt

The primary purpose of /opt is to provide a dedicated location for optional software and add-on applications. Unlike system software that is typically installed in directories like /bin, /sbin, /lib, or /usr, software installed in /opt is often third-party or custom applications that do not conform to the standard filesystem hierarchy.

Self-Contained Software Packages: Applications in /opt often come as complete packages, meaning they contain all necessary files (executables, libraries, configurations) within their own directory structure. This prevents interference with core system files or requiring complex installation procedures.

Isolation: The use of /opt allows software to be installed and updated independently of the core system. This helps prevent version conflicts between system software and third-party applications.

Key Characteristics of /opt

Self-Contained Software: Applications in /opt are typically distributed as complete sets of files, including executables, libraries, and documentation, organized within their own subdirectory.

Third-Party Applications: Many software vendors choose to install their products in /opt, as it provides a clear and isolated location for their applications. This is common with commercial or proprietary software.

Not Essential for Boot: Unlike software in directories like /bin or /usr, the software in /opt is not required for basic system boot or operation. It is considered optional and is typically installed after the system is up and running.

Common Use Cases for /opt

Third-Party Applications: Many commercial or proprietary software packages, such as office suites (e.g., LibreOffice), database systems, and graphics software, are installed in /opt.

Example: /opt/google/chrome for Google Chrome installation.
Example: /opt/lampp for XAMPP, a development environment stack.

Large Software Packages: Complex software packages that include many binaries, libraries, and documentation (e.g., CAD software or enterprise applications) are often installed here.

Example: /opt/idea for JetBrains IntelliJ IDEA.

Software with Special Installation Requirements: Some applications might require a unique directory structure that does not fit into the traditional filesystem hierarchy, and they may choose /opt for installation.

Historical Context

The /opt directory is used to store optional software packages that are not part of the default operating system installation, providing a separate space to install and manage additional software without affecting the core system.

Relationship with Other Directories

/usr vs /opt: The /usr directory typically stores software that is shared across multiple users and is essential to the system. In contrast, /opt is used for optional software, often provided by third-party vendors. While /usr/local is often used for locally compiled software, /opt is typically used for software that is precompiled or packaged in a way that does not conform to the /usr layout.

Self-Contained Nature: Software installed in /opt generally does not require integration with other system binaries and libraries. This differs from software in directories like /usr/bin or /usr/lib, which may need to interact with other system software.

Structure of /opt

The /opt directory is often organized with each package or application installed in its own subdirectory. This structure ensures that each package is self-contained and makes it easy to remove or update individual applications without affecting other software on the system.

Example structure:

/opt/application_name/: Contains all files for a specific application.

/opt/google/chrome/: A subdirectory for Google Chrome's installation.

/opt/lampp/: A subdirectory for the XAMPP stack.
Security Considerations

Permissions: Since software in /opt is typically installed by the system administrator (root), the permissions are usually restricted to prevent unauthorized changes to the software. However, regular users often run the software.

Isolation: The use of /opt ensures that third-party applications are isolated from core system files, which reduces the risk of accidental modification of system-critical files.

Modern Usage

Vendor-Specific Software: Many modern Linux distributions, especially those aimed at enterprise environments, continue to use /opt for software packages from external vendors. This is especially true for large, complex applications that require a specific environment and directory structure.

Flatpak and Snap Packages: With the rise of containerized packaging systems like Flatpak and Snap, software installed through these mechanisms is often placed in a subdirectory within /opt, as these systems are designed to be self-contained and isolated from the rest of the system.

Example: /opt/flatpak/ might contain Flatpak-installed applications.

User-Specific Applications: Although /opt is primarily for system-wide software, some user-installed applications that require complex directory structures might be installed here, though this is less common compared to using other locations like /usr/local.

Summary

The /opt directory is used to house optional third-party software and large add-on packages that are not part of the core operating system. It provides a dedicated space for self-contained applications, which may include their own executables, libraries, and configuration files. This separation helps preserve the integrity of the core system while offering flexibility for installing and managing additional software. By isolating these applications, /opt ensures that they can be easily maintained, updated, and managed independently from the rest of the system, without affecting system stability.

/mnt - Mount points for external devices

The /mnt directory is used to temporarily mount filesystems, such as external drives or network shares, for manual access.

Purpose of /mnt

The primary function of /mnt is to provide a space where external or network-based storage devices can be mounted temporarily. This allows access to data stored on removable media or remote systems, while ensuring that the core file system remains untouched.

Temporary Mounting: /mnt is used for mounting filesystems temporarily, such as a USB drive or a network share.

Not for Persistent Mounting: Unlike /media, which is used for devices that are automatically mounted, /mnt is designed for manual and temporary mounting.

Key Characteristics of /mnt

Temporary: Filesystems mounted in /mnt are usually not persistent and are unmounted when no longer needed.

Manual Mounting: Users or administrators must manually mount filesystems to /mnt using tools like mount.

Not Part of Core OS: The filesystems mounted in /mnt are not required for the system's core functions and are typically not essential for booting.

Common Use Cases for /mnt

Mounting External Storage Devices: USB drives, external hard drives, or CD-ROMs can be mounted to /mnt for short-term access.

Example: mount /dev/sdb1 /mnt/usb

Mounting Network File Systems: Network shares or remote storage can be mounted to /mnt.

Example: mount -t nfs server:/path/to/share /mnt/nfs

Temporary File Access: Disk images or recovery partitions can be mounted here.

Example: mount -o loop disk_image.iso /mnt/iso

Directory Structure
The /mnt directory is usually empty by default. However, subdirectories can be created as needed to mount specific devices or filesystems:

/mnt/usb/: For mounting a USB device.

/mnt/nfs/: For mounting a network share.

Relationship with Other Directories

/media vs /mnt: Both are used for mounting devices, but /mnt is for manually mounted filesystems, whereas /media is used for devices automatically mounted by the system.

Example: /mnt/usb/ is manually mounted, while /media/usb/ is automatically mounted by the system.

/etc/fstab vs /mnt: The /etc/fstab file contains system configurations for automatic mounts, typically for directories like / or /home. However, /mnt is specifically for temporary, manual mounts and is not included in /etc/fstab.

Security Considerations

Mount Permissions: Users need appropriate permissions (e.g., sudo) to mount filesystems in /mnt.

Security Risks with External Devices: It's important to scan external devices for malware before mounting them to prevent potential security threats.

Historical Context
Originally, /mnt was introduced as a temporary mount point for file systems. As Linux distributions evolved, with automatic mounting of devices becoming more common, /mnt was clarified to handle only manual, temporary mounts.

Modern Usage

Backup and Recovery: Administrators often mount recovery partitions or backup volumes in /mnt for restoring or backing up data.

Disk Imaging and Recovery: /mnt is also used to mount disk images (e.g., ISO files) during system recovery.

Virtualization: Virtual disk images or shared directories between host and guest OS in virtualization scenarios may also be mounted here.

Summary
The /mnt directory is a temporary location for manually mounting filesystems, such as external drives, network shares, or disk images. It is primarily used for non-persistent mounts that provide temporary access to external data. Unlike /media, which handles automatic mounting, /mnt is dedicated to manual, temporary mounts and ensures the isolation of these mounts from the core system, simplifying system administration.

/media - Mount points for removable media
The /media directory is used to automatically mount removable media, such as USB drives, CDs, and DVDs, in Linux systems.

Purpose of /media

Automatic Mounting: External devices like USB drives and optical discs are automatically mounted to /media when they are connected, without user intervention.

User Access: Provides an easy way for users to access external storage through predefined subdirectories, typically named after the device label or type (e.g., /media/username/usbdrive).

Key Characteristics

Automounting: The system automatically mounts devices such as USB sticks or DVDs when connected, unlike /mnt for manual mounts.

Device-Specific Subdirectories: Each mounted device has its own subdirectory within /media, named according to the device's label (e.g., /media/username/usbdrive).

Temporary Mounts: Devices are mounted temporarily and unmounted when removed.

Common Use Cases

Mounting USB Devices: When a USB drive is inserted, it is mounted to /media/username/usbdrive for easy access.

Mounting CD/DVDs: Optical media such as CDs and DVDs are automatically mounted to a subdirectory under /media.

Network Shares: Network-mounted file systems may also be mounted to /media.

Directory Structure
Subdirectories in /media are dynamically created when a device is connected, e.g., /media/username/usbdrive/ or /media/username/my-cd/.

Relationship with Other Directories

/mnt vs /media: /mnt is for manually mounted devices, while /media is for automatically mounted devices. For example, /mnt/usb is for manually mounted devices, and /media/username/usbdrive is for automatically mounted ones.

/etc/fstab vs /media: /etc/fstab handles filesystems that are mounted at boot, while /media handles dynamically mounted devices like USBs or CDs.

Security Considerations

Permissions: Only the user who inserted the device typically has full access to the device under /media.

Automounting Risks: Automounting can be a security risk if malicious devices are connected. Some systems may disable it for security reasons.

Unmounting: It's crucial to safely unmount devices from /media to avoid data corruption.

Historical Context

Originally, removable media was mounted manually in directories like /mnt. Over time, /media became the standard for automatically mounted devices in user-friendly environments.

Modern Usage

Graphical File Managers: Desktop environments (GNOME, KDE, Xfce) automatically mount devices to /media and show them in a file manager.

Systemd and Udev: Tools like systemd and udev handle device detection and automatic mounting.

Summary
The /media directory is essential for handling automatically mounted removable devices in Linux. It provides a user-friendly location for accessing external storage without the need for manual intervention. It is an integral part of modern Linux systems, facilitating seamless interaction with removable media.

/dev - Device files for hardware interaction
The /dev directory contains device files that represent hardware and virtual devices, enabling software to interact with them as regular files.

Purpose of /dev
The main purpose of /dev is to provide a uniform interface for accessing hardware. Programs interact with device files (e.g., /dev/sda for a hard disk or /dev/tty for a terminal) to read from and write to hardware without direct manipulation.

Key Characteristics

Character and Block Devices:

Character Devices handle data one character at a time (e.g., /dev/ttyS0 for serial ports).

Block Devices handle data in blocks (e.g., /dev/sda for hard disks).

Permissions: Device files have read, write, and execute permissions, typically restricted to privileged users.

Common Device Files

Block Devices: /dev/sda, /dev/cdrom, /dev/loop0

Character Devices: /dev/tty, /dev/null, /dev/random

Special Devices: /dev/zero, /dev/full, /dev/shm
Virtual Devices: /dev/pts/, /dev/mapper/

Relationship with Other Directories

/sys: Contains kernel information; works with /dev for system control.

/proc: Provides kernel and process information; unlike /dev, it doesn't represent physical or virtual devices.

How /dev Works

udev: Automatically manages device files when hardware is added or removed. It uses rules in /etc/udev/rules.d/ to configure devices dynamically.

Types of Device Files

Block Devices: Represent devices like hard disks (/dev/sda), CD/DVD drives (/dev/cdrom).

Character Devices: Handle devices like keyboards and serial ports (/dev/ttyS0).

Special Devices: Provide special services (/dev/random, /dev/zero).

Security Considerations

Permissions: Device files have permissions to restrict access to root or privileged users to prevent security risks like unauthorized device access.
Risks: Improper handling can expose the system to security vulnerabilities.

Historical Context
In early Unix systems, device files were created manually. With udev, modern Linux systems automatically create and manage these files, making hardware detection and management more flexible.

Modern Usage
Device files are dynamically created and removed by udev. Applications and users interact with devices by referencing device files in /dev (e.g., /dev/sda for hard disk operations).

Summary

The /dev directory is essential for interacting with hardware in Linux. It provides a simple and unified interface for software to communicate with physical and virtual devices, with dynamic management through udev.

/proc - Process and Kernel Information

The /proc directory contains virtual files that provide real-time system information about processes, hardware, and kernel parameters.

Purpose of /proc: The /proc directory is a virtual filesystem in Linux that provides real-time information about the kernel, running processes, memory, hardware, and system configuration. It allows users to interact with the kernel and monitor system activity without consuming physical storage, as the files represent dynamic data generated by the kernel.

Key Characteristics of /proc:

Virtual Filesystem: Files in /proc are not stored on disk but generated dynamically by the kernel.

Read-Only/Read-Write Files: Most files are read-only, but some files can be written to in order to modify kernel parameters.

No Physical Storage: /proc doesn't take up physical disk space; its size depends on system activity.

Common Files and Subdirectories in /proc:

Process Information (/proc/[pid]):
Each running process has a subdirectory identified by its **Process ID (PID), containing files like:**

/proc/[pid]/status: Detailed process information (memory, UID, PID, etc.).

/proc/[pid]/cmdline: Command line that started the process.

/proc/[pid]/fd: Lists open file descriptors.

/proc/[pid]/maps: Shows memory regions used by the process.

System Information:

/proc/cpuinfo: Details about the CPU (type, cores, etc.).

/proc/meminfo: System memory usage (total, free, buffers, etc.).

/proc/version: Kernel version and GCC version.

/proc/uptime: System uptime and idle time.

Kernel Parameters:

/proc/sys: Contains files that can modify kernel parameters for system behavior.

/proc/sys/kernel: Kernel-related settings like hostname, panic parameters, etc.

/proc/sys/vm: Virtual memory management settings.

Hardware Information:

/proc/partitions: Lists disk partitions with sizes.

/proc/interrupts: Information about system interrupts.

/proc/devices: Major/minor numbers for devices on the system.

Networking:

/proc/net: Network-related information (interfaces, routing, connections).

/proc/net/dev: Network interface statistics.

/proc/net/tcp: TCP connection details.

Filesystems and Mounts:

/proc/mounts: Lists currently mounted filesystems.

/proc/filesystems: Lists supported filesystem types.

Important Features of /proc:

Dynamic and Real-Time: /proc provides live system data that updates as the system runs.

Configuration Interface: Some files in /proc can be modified to change kernel behavior.

No Disk Usage: Does not consume physical storage, as it represents virtual data generated by the kernel.

How /proc Works:

Kernel Interaction: /proc is directly integrated with the kernel, offering system-level data and kernel configuration.

Read-Only Access: Most files are for reading system state, while some allow modifications to kernel settings.

Security Considerations:

Access Control: /proc can expose sensitive system data, with access usually restricted to root or privileged users.

Sensitive Data: Process information can expose sensitive details like memory contents and command-line arguments, requiring extra security measures.

Historical Context:
Originally designed to query kernel parameters, /proc evolved into a dynamic system information interface used for process monitoring, system configuration, and debugging.

Modern Usage:

System Monitoring: Administrators and developers use tools like top, ps, and netstat, which rely on /proc to monitor system activity.

Kernel Configuration: The /proc/sys directory allows modification of kernel parameters on-the-fly, without requiring system reboot.

Summary:
The /proc directory is a vital tool for accessing system data, kernel parameters, and process information. Its virtual nature allows dynamic interaction with the system, providing real-time insights and a way to configure the kernel without rebooting. /proc is indispensable for Linux system administration and troubleshooting.

/sys - System device and kernel information

The /sys directory is a virtual filesystem that provides detailed information and configuration options for the kernel, system devices, and hardware.

Purpose of /sys

Device and Driver Information: Exposes data about hardware devices and their associated drivers.

Kernel Configuration: Allows real-time access to kernel settings and the ability to modify them at runtime.

Dynamic Device Tree: Reflects the current state of system devices, dynamically changing as devices are added or removed.

Key Characteristics

Virtual Filesystem: /sys is not a traditional filesystem but a virtual one, where its contents are dynamically generated by the kernel.
Writable Files: Some files can be written to, enabling users to modify kernel parameters or device settings without rebooting.

Device Management: Central for managing devices in Linux, offering a structured interface for device and driver configuration.

Key Subdirectories and Files in /sys

/sys/class: Device Classes
The /sys/class directory categorizes devices by class (type), allowing easy access to their attributes and configurations.

/sys/class/net: Network devices with details like interface names, MAC addresses, and statistics.

/sys/class/block: Information on block devices like hard drives and SSDs, including size and I/O stats.

/sys/class/power_supply: Battery and power source details.

/sys/devices: Device Information

Reflects the system's hardware tree and shows how devices are connected.

/sys/devices/pci0000:00: Contains directories for PCI devices, showing device attributes.

/sys/devices/virtual: Virtual devices that have no physical representation but perform kernel tasks (e.g., CPU).

/sys/kernel: Kernel Settings
This directory provides access to various kernel parameters that influence system behavior.

/sys/kernel/hostname: The system's current hostname.

/sys/kernel/debug: Contains kernel debugging information, requiring debugfs to be enabled.

/sys/firmware: Firmware Information
Exposes information about the system's firmware (BIOS/UEFI) and allows interaction with firmware settings.

/sys/firmware/efi: Details about the EFI system and boot options.

/sys/bus: Information About Device Buses
Provides information on the buses in the system, such as PCI and USB.

/sys/bus/pci: Attributes for devices connected via the PCI bus.

/sys/bus/usb: Information about USB devices.

/sys/fs: Filesystem Information
Contains information about the filesystems in use, such as ext4 or cgroups.

/sys/fs/cgroup: Data about control groups (cgroups), managing resource allocation for groups of processes.

/sys/fs/ext4: Details about the ext4 filesystem, including superblock data.

/sys/module: Kernel Modules
This directory stores information about currently loaded kernel modules.

/sys/module/[module_name]: Subdirectories provide details on specific kernel modules, their parameters, and status.

Important Features of /sys

Dynamic Real-Time Data: As with /proc, /sys is dynamically generated, providing real-time system information.

Writable Files for Configuration: Allows kernel and device parameter adjustments at runtime, such as modifying network MTU or adjusting CPU power settings.

Device Management: Centralized location for device attributes and configurations, essential for hardware management and tuning.

How /sys Works

Kernel Integration: /sys interacts directly with the Linux kernel, providing a dynamic interface for kernel parameters and hardware configuration.

Device and Driver Management: The system updates /sys dynamically as devices are added or removed, reflecting real-time changes.

Security Considerations

Access Control: Since /sys provides sensitive system information, access is typically restricted to root or privileged users. Non-privileged users may be restricted in what they can modify.

Potential Risks: Modifying certain files can affect system stability and hardware management, so caution is advised when making changes.

Historical Context
The /sys directory was introduced as part of the sysfs virtual filesystem to provide a structured, unified interface for interacting with kernel parameters and hardware devices. Over time, it has become a critical component for system management.

Modern Usage

Device Management: /sys allows for real-time management of hardware devices, making it essential for system administrators and developers.

Kernel Tuning: Administrators can fine-tune kernel behavior and system performance by modifying parameters in /sys.

Monitoring: Tools like udevadm, sysctl, and lsmod interact with /sys to gather system status and apply real-time adjustments.

Summary
The /sys directory is a crucial component of the Linux filesystem, providing a dynamic interface for interacting with kernel settings, hardware devices, and system parameters. By offering real-time data and writable configuration files, /sys enables efficient device management, system tuning, and hardware monitoring, making it indispensable for Linux system administration and development.

/boot - Boot Loader and Kernel Files
The /boot directory stores essential files for booting the Linux system, including the kernel, bootloader configurations, and initrd images.

Purpose of /boot
The /boot directory is where critical files for the boot process are stored. It includes the kernel, bootloader files, and the initrd, which helps mount the root filesystem. These files allow the system to start up and load the operating system.

Key Characteristics of /boot

Bootloader Files: Files that help load the OS, such as GRUB configurations.

Kernel Images: Compressed Linux kernel files loaded during boot.

Initrd/initramfs: Temporary filesystem stored in RAM to load drivers and other essential components.

Fixed Location: /boot contents usually remain static and do not change often during system operation.

Key Subdirectories and Files in /boot

/boot/grub: GRUB Bootloader Files

/boot/grub/grub.cfg: Main GRUB configuration file for boot settings.

/boot/grub2/: Some distributions may use /boot/grub2/ for GRUB-related files.

/boot/vmlinuz-*: Linux Kernel Image

/boot/vmlinuz-<version>: The compressed Linux kernel image. Multiple kernel versions may be stored here for fallback.

/boot/initrd.img-*: Initial RAM Disk

/boot/initrd.img-<version>: Compressed image used to load necessary components for booting the system.

/boot/System.map-*: Kernel Symbol Table
/boot/System.map-<version>: Contains mappings of kernel functions and variables to memory addresses, useful for debugging.

/boot/config-*: Kernel Configuration
/boot/config-<version>: Configuration file for building the kernel, including enabled features.

/boot/splash/*: Boot Splash Screens (optional)

/boot/splash/: Contains files for graphical boot screens, if enabled.

How /boot Fits Into the Boot Process

Power On: BIOS or UEFI firmware initializes hardware and loads the bootloader.

Bootloader Loads: GRUB reads its configuration from /boot/grub/grub.cfg to present boot options.

Kernel and Initrd Loading: GRUB loads the kernel and initrd images into memory.

Kernel Execution: The kernel starts, decompresses, and initializes hardware.

System Initialization: The kernel hands control to the init process, continuing the system startup.

Security Considerations

Root Privileges: /boot is usually restricted to root users to prevent unauthorized changes that could make the system unbootable.

Space Management: If /boot is on a separate partition, old kernel versions can take up space. It's recommended to clean up old kernels periodically.

Typical /boot Directory Structure
/boot/

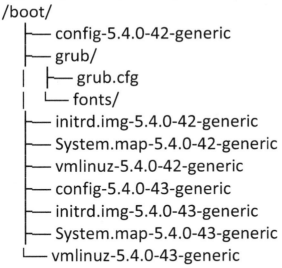

```
/boot/
    ├── config-5.4.0-42-generic
    ├── grub/
    │    ├── grub.cfg
    │    └── fonts/
    ├── initrd.img-5.4.0-42-generic
    ├── System.map-5.4.0-42-generic
    ├── vmlinuz-5.4.0-42-generic
    ├── config-5.4.0-43-generic
    ├── initrd.img-5.4.0-43-generic
    ├── System.map-5.4.0-43-generic
    └── vmlinuz-5.4.0-43-generic
```

Summary

The /boot directory is crucial for booting a Linux system. It contains kernel images, bootloader configurations, the initial RAM disk, and other necessary files to boot the system and mount the root filesystem. Proper management of the /boot directory, such as cleaning up old kernel files, is essential for system stability and security.

/run - Runtime Data and System State

The /run directory stores temporary runtime data essential for system processes, services, and inter-process communication, cleared on shutdown or reboot.

Purpose of /run

The /run directory is intended for storing volatile data that is necessary only during the current session. It includes information about running processes, system state, and other temporary files needed during the system's uptime. Once the system is rebooted, this data is erased.

Key Characteristics:

Volatile Storage: Data in /run does not persist beyond reboots, unlike /var, which holds persistent data.

System-Specific Data: Contains runtime information required for system services and inter-process communication.

Temporary State Information: Provides space for quick access files that do not need to be stored long-term.

Key Subdirectories and Files in /run

/run/lock: Lock Files
Used to prevent conflicting access to resources by different processes. Lock files ensure that only one process can access a resource (e.g., a file or device) at a time.

/run/user/<UID>: User-Specific Runtime Files
Each user has a directory under /run/user/ to store data related to their session, including process information, sockets, and session-specific data.

/run/systemd: Systemd Runtime Data
Holds runtime data related to systemd, the init system for many modern Linux distributions. This includes information about services, logs, and unit states.

/run/sockets: IPC Sockets
Stores Unix domain socket files for inter-process communication (IPC) between services and applications.

/run/initramfs: Initramfs Runtime Data
Contains temporary files used during the early stages of boot, specifically before the root filesystem is mounted.

/run/shm: Shared Memory
Provides shared memory space for applications, allowing for fast, in-memory communication between processes.

How /run Fits Into the System

System Services: Services store and access runtime data in /run for managing system state and inter-service communication.

Process Communication: IPC is handled through socket files stored in /run/sockets, enabling efficient communication between processes.

Locking and Synchronization: Lock files in /run/lock help prevent conflicts by ensuring exclusive access to resources.

User-Specific Data: The /run/user/<UID> directories track individual user sessions and processes.

Security Considerations

Permissions: Generally, only the root user or specific services have write access to /run, safeguarding system-level data.

Temporary Nature: Sensitive data should not be stored in /run, as it is cleared upon reboot. Security-critical data should go in more permanent directories like /etc or /var.

Typical /run Directory Structure

```
/run/
    ├── lock/
    │   └── somefile.lock
    ├── user/
    │   ├── 1000/
    │   │   ├── lock/
    │   │   └── systemd/
```

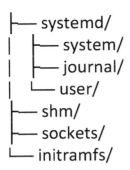

```
├── systemd/
│   ├── system/
│   ├── journal/
│   └── user/
├── shm/
├── sockets/
└── initramfs/
```

Summary
The /run directory is a vital component of the Linux filesystem, designed to store temporary, volatile runtime data necessary for system operation. This includes lock files, user session data, IPC sockets, and systemd's runtime data. Although essential for the system's smooth operation, the contents of /run are cleared upon reboot, ensuring that only session-relevant information is retained.

/srv - Data for services provided by the system

The /srv directory stores data served by system services, such as web, FTP, and database servers, providing content shared with clients or other systems.

Purpose of /srv
/srv stores service-specific data required by the system's server processes. This includes files being shared by web servers, file servers, FTP servers, and more. The purpose is to centralize service-related files that need to be accessed by system daemons.

Key Characteristics of /srv

Service-Specific Data: Designed exclusively for files served by system services, distinguishing it from directories like /var that hold variable data.

Accessible to Services: Files in /srv are accessed by system processes (e.g., Apache, NFS) that provide services to clients.

Service Organization: The structure within /srv is organized by service type, making it easy to manage and locate service-specific data.

Key Subdirectories in /srv

Web Server Data (/srv/www)
Stores files served by web servers (e.g., Apache, Nginx), such as HTML files and assets.

/srv/www/html: Main directory for public-facing website content.

/srv/www/cgi-bin: Stores CGI scripts for dynamic web content.

FTP Server Data (/srv/ftp)
Contains files made available for FTP clients to upload or download.

/srv/ftp: Directory for FTP data, often organized by users or projects.

File Server Data (/srv/nfs)

Used for systems running NFS or other network file sharing protocols.

/srv/nfs: Contains shared directories or files for clients accessing network resources.

Git Repository Data (/srv/git)
Stores Git repositories or version-controlled projects for systems hosting Git services.

/srv/git: Directory for Git repository data.

Database Server Data (/srv/mysql or /srv/postgresql)
Stores database files for systems like MySQL or PostgreSQL.

/srv/mysql: For MySQL database files.

/srv/postgresql: For PostgreSQL database files.

Other Services
Other services may also have data stored in /srv, such as:

/srv/minecraft: Data for Minecraft servers.

/srv/mail: Email service data, such as queues or messages.

/srv/media: Media content for media servers.

How /srv Fits Into the System

Service Data Centralization: Helps keep data for all system services organized, with specific directories for each service type (e.g., /srv/www for web server data).

User and System Data Separation: Keeps service data separate from user data (/home) and variable data (/var), aiding in easier management.

Standardized Location for Service Files: Provides a consistent, centralized location for all service data, making configuration and maintenance easier for administrators.

Security Considerations

Permissions: Proper permissions are essential for securing /srv, especially since it contains data shared with clients. Web server files should be publicly readable but not writable by unauthorized users.

Data Separation: Each service's data should have its own subdirectory within /srv with correct user/group permissions.

Backup and Redundancy: As /srv holds critical service data, it should be regularly backed up to avoid data loss.

Example Directory Structure for /srv

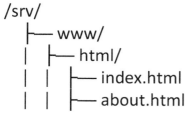

```
/srv/
    ├── www/
    │   ├── html/
    │   │   ├── index.html
    │   │   ├── about.html
```

```
|   ├── cgi-bin/
|   |   └── script.cgi
├── ftp/
|   ├── incoming/
|   ├── outgoing/
├── nfs/
|   ├── share1/
|   └── share2/
├── mysql/
|   ├── database1/
|   ├── database2/
├── git/
|   ├── repo1.git/
|   └── repo2.git/
├── media/
|   ├── movie1.mp4
|   └── movie2.mp4
```

Summary

The /srv directory is essential for organizing data that is provided or served by system services, such as web servers, FTP servers, and databases. It centralizes service-specific files, ensuring that these critical resources are easily accessible and properly managed. With its well-defined structure and security considerations, /srv plays a key role in maintaining the functionality and security of Linux-based systems.

/lost+found - Recovered files from file system errors

The /lost+found directory stores recovered files that have been fragmented or corrupted, typically after a system crash or improper shutdown, helping maintain file system integrity.

Purpose of /lost+found

The /lost+found directory serves as a designated area for files that the file system has recovered after an error or crash. These files may have become "orphaned" (i.e., they no longer have an associated directory entry) due to unexpected shutdowns or other system failures. The directory helps to recover and manage these files, even if they cannot be restored to their original location or path.

Key Characteristics of /lost+found

File Recovery: Stores fragmented or corrupted files that have been orphaned due to file system issues like crashes or improper shutdowns.

System Integrity: Ensures that files with lost directory entries are still recoverable, maintaining overall file system health.

Access Control: Typically, only system administrators (root) have access to /lost+found, as it may contain incomplete or sensitive data.

How Files End Up in /lost+found

Files can end up in /lost+found after a system crash or file system corruption is detected during a file system check (fsck). The fsck utility scans for orphaned files—those that are not associated with a valid directory—and places them in this special directory for further inspection.

Examples of situations that cause files to end up in /lost+found:

Power Failure or System Crash: Files being written to disk may become orphaned if the system shuts down unexpectedly.

Unclean File System Unmount: Improperly unmounting a file system can leave files in an inconsistent state.

Corruption or Disk Errors: Errors like bad sectors or other corruption can result in files losing their directory references.

Files in /lost+found
Files placed in /lost+found typically do not have meaningful names. Instead, they are assigned cryptic names like #1234, based on the file's inode number.
The system administrator must manually inspect and recover these files, which might involve renaming, restoring, or relocating them.

Naming Convention:
Files are named using the inode number (e.g., #1234), which corresponds to the file's location in the file system.
These files may need to be examined and re-associated with the appropriate directories by the system administrator.

Manual Recovery:

Inspecting Files: Use tools like file or hexdump to identify the file type and contents.

Renaming and Recovering: Once identified, files should be renamed and placed back in their correct directories.

Data Integrity: Ensure that recovered files are intact and not corrupted before reintegrating them into the system.

How It Works

fsck Utility: When you run fsck on a file system (either during boot or manually), the utility scans for inconsistencies and orphaned files.

File Movement: Any orphaned files discovered by fsck are moved to /lost+found for recovery.

File Restoration: In some cases, fsck can restore files to their original locations. If this is not possible, the files remain in /lost+found for manual inspection.

Default Location

Location: The /lost+found directory is located in the root directory (/) of each file system partition.

Creation: It is automatically created when a file system (e.g., ext2, ext3, or ext4) is formatted, and it may also be created manually if necessary.

Permissions and Access
Typically, the /lost+found directory is owned by the root user.
Regular users generally do not have access to /lost+found because it contains fragmented and potentially sensitive data.

How to Handle Files in /lost+found
If you find files in /lost+found, here's what to do:

Inspect the Files: Use commands like file or hexdump to determine the file type and contents.

Rename and Recover: Once identified, move the file to a proper directory and rename it to something recognizable.

Verify Data Integrity: Check that the recovered file is complete and not corrupted before using it.

Example Directory Structure for /lost+found
```
/lost+found/
       ├── #1234  (Recovered file, may need to be inspected)
       ├── #5678  (Recovered file, fragmented data)
       ├── #9101  (Recovered file, might be part of a larger file)
```

Summary

The /lost+found directory is a critical feature of Linux file systems like ext2, ext3, and ext4. It serves as a recovery space for files that have been orphaned due to system crashes, corruption, or improper shutdowns. Through the fsck utility, these files are recovered and placed in /lost+found, where system administrators can inspect and recover them. While /lost+found is crucial for maintaining file system integrity, it often requires manual intervention to identify and restore the recovered files properly.

Navigation Commands

Navigating the filesystem is fundamental when working in a Linux environment. Here are some of the most commonly used commands for basic navigation:

cd (Change Directory)
The cd command is used to move between directories in the file system. It allows you to change the current working directory to another location.

Usage: cd /path/to/directory

To move to the parent directory (one level up):
cd ..

To go directly to your home directory:

cd ~

ls (List Directory Contents)
The ls command lists the files and directories within the current directory or a specified path.

Usage: ls

Common options include:
ls -l: Displays detailed information about files, including permissions, ownership, size, and modification date.

ls -a: Shows hidden files (those that start with a dot).

ls -h: Makes the file sizes human-readable (in KB, MB, etc.).

pwd (Print Working Directory)
The pwd command displays the full path of the current directory you are in. It's useful to know exactly where you are in the file system at any time.

Usage: pwd

This will return something like:
/home/username/Documents

tree (Directory Tree View)
The tree command displays the directory structure of the current directory or a specified directory in a tree-like format. It's a great way to visually understand the hierarchy of files and folders.

Usage: tree

If you want to display only the directories (and omit files), you can use:
tree -d

If tree is not installed by default, you can install it using your package manager, such as:
sudo apt install tree # For Debian/Ubuntu-based systems
sudo yum install tree # For Red Hat/CentOS-based systems

du (Disk Usage)
The du command is used to check the disk space usage of files and directories. It's helpful when you need to understand how much space specific files or directories are consuming.

Usage: du /path/to/directory

Common options include:

du -h: Displays sizes in a human-readable format.

du -sh: Shows only the total size of the specified directory.

du -a: Includes all files, not just directories, in the output.

pushd and popd (Directory Stack Navigation)

These commands allow you to work with a stack of directories, making it easy to jump between different directories without losing track of where you were.

pushd: Saves your current directory in a stack and moves you to a new one.

Usage: pushd /path/to/directory

This adds the current directory to the stack and changes the working directory to /path/to/directory.

popd: Returns you to the directory at the top of the stack (the one you previously saved using pushd).

Usage: popd

This pops the top directory off the stack and changes the working directory to that location.

find (Search for Files and Directories)

The find command searches the directory tree to find files and directories based on a given pattern or condition. It is incredibly powerful for locating files without knowing their exact location.

Usage: find /path/to/search -name "filename"

Some common options:

-name: Search for files by name.

-type d: Search for directories.

-type f: Search for files.
-size +100M: Find files larger than 100MB.

Example:
find /home -type f -name "*.txt"

This searches for all .txt files in the /home directory.

locate (Quick File Search)
The locate command is a quicker way to find files by name, but it works differently from find because it relies on a pre-built database of files (typically updated periodically by the system).

Usage: locate filename

Before using locate, you might need to update the file database with:

sudo updated

---

locate is faster than find because it searches a database rather than the live filesystem, but the results may not always be up-to-date.

stat (File/Directory Status)

The stat command provides detailed information about a file or directory, such as its size, permissions, inode number, and timestamps for creation, modification, and access.

Usage: stat filename

Example output:
File: 'filename'
Size: 1024   Blocks: 8   IO Block: 4096 regular file
Device: 803h/2051d Inode: 1234567   Links: 1
Access: (0644/-rw-r--r--)   Uid: (1000/username)   Gid: (1000/username)
Access: 2024-11-21 10:30:00.000000000
Modify: 2024-11-21 10:00:00.000000000
Change: 2024-11-21 10:05:00.000000000

df (Disk Free Space)

The df command shows the amount of disk space used and available on filesystems.

Usage: df

Common options:

df -h: Displays sizes in a human-readable format (MB, GB).

df -T: Shows the filesystem type (e.g., ext4, xfs).

basename and dirname (Extracting File Path Components)
These commands allow you to extract the directory or filename from a given path.

basename: Returns just the filename from a path.

Usage: basename /path/to/file.txt

Output: file.txt

dirname: Returns just the directory from a path.

Usage: dirname /path/to/file.txt

Output: /path/to

head and tail (View Beginning or End of a File)
head: Shows the first few lines of a file (default is 10 lines).

Usage: head filename

tail: Shows the last few lines of a file (default is 10 lines). You can also use tail to monitor a file in real-time, such as log files, with the -f option.

Usage: tail -f filename

history (Command History)

The history command displays a list of commands you've recently executed. You can use this to review or rerun previous commands.

Usage: history

You can also run a specific command from history by referencing its number:

!123

This would re-run command number 123 from the history.

grep (Search Within Files)

The grep command is used to search text or patterns within files. It's handy for finding specific lines of text or patterns across files.

Usage: grep "search_term" filename

Options:

grep -r "search_term" /path/to/directory: Recursively search for a term in all files in a directory.

grep -i: Case-insensitive search.

xargs (Run Commands on Output)

The xargs command is used to build and execute commands from standard input. It's especially useful in combination with other commands like find.

Usage: find /path/to/directory -name "*.txt" | xargs rm

This example finds all .txt files in the specified directory and then deletes them using rm.

File and Directory Management Commands

File and directory management in Linux involves commands to create, move, copy, delete, and organize files and directories. Commands like cp (copy), mv (move/rename), and rm (remove) handle file operations, while mkdir (make directory) and rmdir (remove directory) manage directories. The touch command creates empty files or updates timestamps, providing essential tools for maintaining an organized file system.

cp (Copy)

Copies files or directories.
Usage: cp source destination
Example: cp file1.txt file2.txt (copies file1.txt to file2.txt)

mv (Move/Rename)
Moves or renames files or directories.
Usage: mv source destination
Example: mv oldname.txt newname.txt (renames oldname.txt to newname.txt).

rm (Remove)
Deletes files or directories.
Usage: rm filename
Example: rm file.txt (removes file.txt).
Note: Use rm -r to remove directories.

mkdir (Make Directory)
Creates a new directory.
Usage: mkdir directory_name
Example: mkdir new_folder (creates a directory named new_folder).

rmdir (Remove Directory)
Removes an empty directory.
Usage: rmdir directory_name
Example: rmdir old_folder (removes old_folder if it's empty).

touch (Create/Update File)
Creates an empty file if it doesn't exist, or updates the timestamp of an existing file.
Usage: touch filename
Example: touch newfile.txt (creates newfile.txt or updates its timestamp).

ln (Create Link)
Creates hard or symbolic links to files or directories.
Usage: ln target link_name (for hard links), ln -s target link_name (for symbolic links).
Example: ln -s /path/to/original /path/to/link (creates a symbolic link to the original file).

find (Search Files)
Searches for files and directories based on specific criteria.
Usage: find path -options
Example: find /home -name "*.txt" (finds all .txt files in the /home directory).

chmod (Change Permissions)
Modifies file or directory permissions.
Usage: chmod permissions filename

Example: chmod 755 file.txt (sets the permissions of file.txt).

chown (Change Ownership)
Changes the owner and/or group of a file or directory.
Usage: chown owner:group filename
Example: chown user:group file.txt (changes the ownership of file.txt).

df (Disk Space Usage)
Displays information about available disk space on mounted filesystems.
Usage: df -h
Example: df -h (shows disk usage in human-readable format).

du (Disk Usage)
Shows the disk usage of files and directories.
Usage: du -sh directory_name
Example: du -sh /home/user (shows the total disk usage of the /home/user directory).

stat (Display File or File System Status)
Displays detailed information about a file or directory.

Usage: stat filename
Example: stat file.txt (displays details like size, permissions, and modification date).

rename (Rename Multiple Files)
Renames multiple files using patterns.
Usage: rename 's/old_pattern/new_pattern/' files
Example: rename 's/.txt/.md/' *.txt (renames all .txt files to .md).

Permission and Ownership Commands
Permissions and ownership in Linux govern access to files and directories, ensuring that only authorized users and processes can read, write, or execute them. Each file and directory has an owner, a group, and a set of permissions that define what actions can be performed by different users. The owner typically has full control over the file, while others may have read, write, or execute permissions, depending on the settings. These permissions are represented as a combination of letters (r, w, x) or numbers (in octal format) and can be modified using commands like chmod (to change permissions), chown (to change ownership), and chgrp (to change group ownership). Properly setting permissions is crucial for system security and user privacy.

chmod (Change Permissions)

Changes the read, write, and execute permissions of files or directories.

Usage: chmod [options] permissions filename

Summary of Key Options:

-R: Recursively apply permissions to a directory and its contents.

-v: Verbose output to show which permissions are being modified.

-c: Output only when permissions are changed.

--reference: Set permissions to match another file.

Examples:

chmod 755 file.txt (gives the owner full permissions and others read-execute permissions).

chmod u+x file.sh (adds execute permission for the user).

chown (Change Ownership)

Changes the owner and/or group of a file or directory.

Usage: chown owner[:group] filename

Examples:

chown user:group file.txt (changes the owner of file.txt to user and the group to group).

chown user file.txt (changes only the owner of file.txt to user).

chgrp (Change Group Ownership)
Changes the group ownership of a file or directory.

Usage: chgrp group filename
Example: chgrp admin file.txt (changes the group of file.txt to admin).

umask (Set Default Permissions)
Sets the default file permissions for newly created files and directories.

Usage: umask [mask]

Example: umask 022 (sets default permissions of newly created files to 755 and directories to 755).

getfacl (Get File Access Control List)
Displays the file access control list (ACL) of a file or directory, which can provide more granular permission settings than standard file permissions.

Usage: getfacl filename

Example: getfacl file.txt (displays the ACL for file.txt).

setfacl (Set File Access Control List)
Sets or modifies the access control list (ACL) of a file or directory.
Usage: setfacl -m u:user:permissions filename

Example: setfacl -m u:user:rw file.txt (gives user read-write permissions on file.txt).

ls -l (List Files with Detailed Information)
Lists files and directories with detailed information, including permissions and ownership.

Usage: ls -l

Example: ls -l (shows file permissions, owner, group, and other file details).

sudo (Superuser Do)
Executes commands with superuser (root) privileges, allowing users to change ownership or modify protected files.

Usage: sudo command

Example: sudo chown root file.txt (changes ownership of file.txt to root).

stat (Display File Status)
Displays detailed information about a file, including permissions, ownership, and timestamps.

Usage: stat filename

Example: stat file.txt (displays detailed information about file.txt, including permissions and owner).

acl (Access Control Lists Management)
Manages extended ACLs for fine-grained permission control (often used with getfacl and setfacl).

Usage: Various tools to manage ACL, like getfacl for reading and setfacl for writing.

Example: getfacl file.txt (reads the ACL of file.txt).

chcon (Change SELinux Context)
Changes the SELinux security context of files and directories.

Usage: chcon [options] context filename

Example: chcon -t httpd_sys_content_t file.txt (changes the SELinux context of file.txt for use by the HTTP server).

semanage (SELinux Management)
Manages SELinux policies, including file contexts and booleans.

Usage: semanage fcontext -a -t context filename

Example: semanage fcontext -a -t httpd_sys_content_t /var/www/html (sets the SELinux context for /var/www/html to httpd_sys_content_t).

setenforce (Set SELinux Mode)
Temporarily sets the SELinux mode (enforcing or permissive).

Usage: setenforce [0 | 1]

Example: setenforce 1 (sets SELinux to enforcing mode).

restorecon (Restore SELinux Context)
Restores the SELinux security context of files based on the system's default policy.

Usage: restorecon -v filename

Example: restorecon -v /var/www/html (restores the default SELinux context for the web directory).

newgrp (Change Group ID)
Changes the user's current group to a specified group, which is useful for managing file permissions within different groups.

Usage: newgrp groupname

Example: newgrp admin (changes the current group to admin for the user).

umask (Set File Creation Mask)
Sets the default permissions for new files and directories. It determines what permissions are *not* granted when creating new files.

Usage: umask [mask]

Example: umask 022 (sets the default file permissions so new files have 644 and directories 755).

lsattr (List File Attributes)

Lists the attributes of files, which are special flags used to control certain characteristics of files (like immutability).

Usage: lsattr filename

Example: lsattr file.txt (shows the attributes of file.txt).

chattr (Change File Attributes)

Changes the file attributes that control aspects like immutability, append-only mode, etc.

Usage: chattr [options] filename

Example: chattr +i file.txt (marks file.txt as immutable, preventing any modifications).

auditctl (Control Audit System)

Configures the Linux audit subsystem to track and record file access and changes, which is useful for auditing file and directory access.

Usage: auditctl -w filename -p action

Example: auditctl -w /etc/passwd -p wa (sets up auditing for writes and attribute changes on /etc/passwd).

ausearch (Search Audit Logs)

Searches the audit logs for specific events related to file and directory access.

Usage: ausearch -f filename

Example: ausearch -f /etc/passwd (searches the audit logs for access to /etc/passwd).

auditd (Audit Daemon)

The daemon that collects and writes audit records, which can include detailed access information for files and directories.

Usage: service auditd start

Example: service auditd start (starts the audit daemon to begin tracking file and directory access).

Creating and Managing Symbolic Links: (Soft & Hard)

Creating and managing links in Linux involves two main types: symbolic (soft) links and hard links. Symbolic links are essentially shortcuts or pointers to files or directories, and they can span across different file systems. They store the target's path, and if the target is deleted, the symbolic link becomes broken. They are created using the ln -s command. On the other hand, hard links directly reference a file's inode, making them indistinguishable from the original file. Both the hard link and the original file share the same data, so even if one is deleted, the data remains accessible through the other. Hard links can only be created within the same file system and are created using the ln command. While symbolic links are ideal for linking across file systems or for directories, hard links are useful for creating redundant file references and ensuring data persistence within a file system.

ln -s [target] [link_name]
Description:
ln -s: The command to create a symbolic (soft) link.
[target]: The file or directory you want to create a link to.
[link_name]: The name of the symbolic link you want to create.

When to use symbolic links:

Cross-file system links: Symbolic links can span different file systems, whereas hard links are limited to the same file system.

Shortcut creation: Symbolic links act as pointers or shortcuts to a target file or directory, making it easier to reference files located in different directories without moving or copying them.

Improved organization: Symbolic links allow you to organize files and directories in a more logical or accessible way without duplicating data.

Configuration files: Often used in configuration file management (e.g., linking /etc/nginx/nginx.conf to a custom configuration file for easier management).

Example: Creating a symbolic link to a file:
ln -s /path/to/original/file.txt /path/to/link_name.txt
This creates a symbolic link named link_name.txt pointing to file.txt.

Example: Creating a symbolic link to a directory:
ln -s /home/user/documents /home/user/docs_link

ln [target] [link_name]

Description:
ln: The command to create a hard link.
[target]: The file to which you want to create a hard link.

[link_name]: The name of the hard link you want to create.

When to use hard links:

Same file system: Hard links can only be created within the same file system. Unlike symbolic links, hard links don't reference the file by its name but by its inode (the actual data block on the disk).

Multiple references to the same data: Hard links allow multiple references to the same file content. Deleting one link does not remove the data as long as another hard link to it exists.

File redundancy: Hard links can be useful for creating redundant references to the same file, ensuring that the data remains accessible even if one reference is removed.

Data integrity: Since both the original file and the hard link point to the same inode, they are identical and changes made to one will affect the other.

Example: Creating a hard link to a file:
ln /path/to/original/file.txt /path/to/hard_link.txt
This creates a hard link hard_link.txt that points to the same data as file.txt. Both file.txt and hard_link.txt share the same inode, and deleting one will not delete the data if the other link still exists.

Differences from Symbolic Links:

File content: Hard links point directly to the file's data (inode), making the link indistinguishable from the original file, while symbolic links point to the file's pathname.

File system constraints: Hard links cannot span different file systems, while symbolic links can.

Link behavior: Deleting the original file in a hard link setup does not remove the data as long as the hard link exists, whereas deleting a symbolic link does not affect the original file.

Chapter 2: Working with Files

Working with files in Linux involves navigating the filesystem, managing file permissions, and utilizing command-line tools to create, read, edit, and delete files. Linux treats everything as a file, including hardware devices and system resources, making file management integral to system operation.

Key commands like touch, cat, cp, mv, and rm are used to handle files, while permissions and ownership are managed through commands like chmod and chown. Understanding file types, directory structures, and symbolic links is essential for efficient file operations in Linux. Additionally, powerful text editors like vim or nano allow users to edit files directly from the terminal, making file manipulation flexible and efficient.

Viewing and Editing Files

Viewing and editing files in Linux can be done using various command-line tools, each designed for specific tasks. The cat command (short for concatenate) is used to display the contents of a file in the terminal, making it useful for quick viewing. However, for larger files, less and more are more appropriate. Both allow you to scroll through files one screen at a time, but less offers more advanced navigation, like scrolling backwards, while more is simpler but only allows forward movement. The head and tail commands are used to view specific portions of a file; head displays the first few lines, while tail shows the last few. These commands are particularly useful for monitoring logs or quickly checking parts of files without loading the entire content.

cat
Display the entire content of a file:
cat filename.txt
Example: cat notes.txt
This will output all the contents of notes.txt in the terminal.

less
View the contents of a file with scrollable navigation (both forward and backward):
less filename.txt
Example: less largefile.txt
This allows you to scroll through largefile.txt with arrow keys, q to quit.

more
View the content of a file, one screen at a time (only scroll forward):
more filename.txt
Example: more log.txt
This will display the content of log.txt one screen at a time. Press Space to move to the next screen, or q to quit.

head
View the first 10 lines of a file by default:
head filename.txt

Example: head -n 5 data.txt

This will show the first 5 lines of data.txt. The -n option lets you specify the number of lines.

tail

View the last 10 lines of a file by default:

tail filename.txt

Example: tail -n 20 server.log

This will display the last 20 lines of server.log.

You can also use the -f option to follow the file in real-time (useful for monitoring logs):

tail -f server.log

This will keep displaying new lines as they are added to server.log.

File Manipulation

File manipulation in Linux involves managing files and directories using various commands. The cp command is used to copy files or directories from one location to another, preserving the original file. For example, cp file.txt /path/to/destination creates a duplicate of file.txt. The mv command is used to move or rename files and directories; for instance, mv oldname.txt newname.txt renames a file, while moving is done by specifying a different destination. The rm command removes files or directories, such as rm file.txt for files or rm -r folder for directories (with -r for recursive deletion). The ln command is used to create links. Symbolic links (ln -s target linkname) act as pointers to a file or directory, while hard links (ln target linkname) directly reference the file's inode, allowing it to exist in multiple locations without duplicating the data. These tools provide flexibility for organizing, moving, and deleting files within the Linux filesystem.

cp

Copy a file or directory:
cp source.txt /path/to/destination/

Example: cp report.txt /home/user/documents/
This copies report.txt to the /home/user/documents/ directory.

Copying a directory (with the -r option for recursive):
cp -r /path/to/source_dir /path/to/destination_dir

Example: cp -r /home/user/photos /backup/
This copies the entire photos directory to the /backup/ directory.

mv

Move or rename a file or directory:
mv oldname.txt newname.txt
Example: mv draft.txt final.txt
This renames draft.txt to final.txt.

Moving a file to a different directory:
mv file.txt /home/user/newlocation/

Example: mv file.txt /home/user/documents/
This moves file.txt to the /home/user/documents/ directory.

rm

Remove files or directories:
rm filename.txt

Example: rm old_report.txt
This deletes the file old_report.txt.

To remove a directory and its contents, use the recursive option -r:

rm -r /path/to/directory

Example: rm -r /home/user/tempfiles/
This removes the entire tempfiles directory and its contents.

ln

Create symbolic and hard links:

Symbolic link (shortcut to another file or directory):
ln -s /path/to/target /path/to/linkname

Example:
 ln -s /home/user/original.txt /home/user/link_to_original.txt
This creates a symbolic link link_to_original.txt that points to original.txt.

Hard link (a direct reference to the file's inode):
ln /path/to/target /path/to/linkname

Example:
ln /home/user/file.txt /home/user/hardlink_file.txt

This creates a hard link hardlink_file.txt that directly references the same inode as file.txt, essentially creating two references to the same file without duplicating data.

Text Search and Manipulation

Text search and manipulation in Linux is efficiently handled using powerful command-line tools like grep, sed, awk, cut, sort, uniq, and diff. The grep command searches files for patterns or specific strings, making it ideal for finding information quickly. sed (stream editor) allows for text manipulation and transformation, such as search-and-replace within files. awk is a versatile text processing tool used for pattern scanning and data extraction, especially in structured data formats like CSV. The cut command extracts specific columns or fields from files, while sort arranges lines of text in a specified order. uniq filters out repeated lines, often used in combination with sort. The diff command compares the contents of two files and highlights their differences, making it valuable for tracking changes. Together, these tools allow users to perform complex text processing and data manipulation tasks directly from the terminal, streamlining workflows and automating tasks.

grep

Search for a pattern in a file:
grep "search_term" filename.txt

Example: grep "error" log.txt

This searches for the word "error" in log.txt and prints all matching lines.

To search recursively in a directory:
grep -r "search_term" /path/to/directory

sed

Search and replace text in a file:
sed 's/old_text/new_text/g' filename.txt

Example: sed 's/foo/bar/g' data.txt
This replaces all occurrences of "foo" with "bar" in data.txt.

To make changes directly to the file:
sed -i 's/old_text/new_text/g' filename.txt

awk

Extract and process data from a file:
awk '{print $1, $3}' filename.txt

Example: awk '{print $2}' employees.txt
This prints the second field (e.g., a column of data) from each line in employees.txt.

You can also apply conditions:
awk '$3 > 1000 {print $1, $3}' sales.txt
This prints the first and third columns for rows where the third column is greater than 1000.

cut
Extract specific columns from a file:
cut -d' ' -f1,3 filename.txt
Example: cut -d',' -f2 students.csv
This extracts the second column from a CSV file students.csv
using a comma (,) as the delimiter.

sort

Sort the lines of a file:
sort filename.txt

Example:
sort names.txt
This sorts the lines in names.txt alphabetically.

To sort numerically:
sort -n numbers.txt

uniq

Remove duplicate lines from a file:
uniq filename.txt

Example: sort log.txt | uniq

This sorts log.txt first, then removes duplicate lines.

To count occurrences of unique lines:
sort log.txt | uniq -c

diff

Compare two files and show their differences:
diff file1.txt file2.txt

Example: diff original.txt modified.txt
This shows the differences between original.txt and modified.txt.

You can use -u for a unified format that's easier to read:
diff -u original.txt modified.txt

Compressing & Decompressing Files

Compressing files in Linux is commonly done using tools like tar, gzip, bzip2, zip, and unzip. The tar command is used to archive multiple files and directories into a single file, often referred to as a "tarball," without compression by default. Compression can be added by combining tar with gzip (resulting in a .tar.gz file) or bzip2 (creating a .tar.bz2 file), which offer different levels of compression efficiency. The gzip and bzip2 commands are used individually to compress single files, with bzip2 typically providing better compression but being slower. The zip command compresses files into .zip format, which is widely used and compatible across various platforms, while unzip extracts the contents of a .zip archive. These tools help reduce file size for storage and transmission, making them essential for managing large datasets or backups in Linux environments.

tar

Create an archive (without compression):
tar -cvf archive.tar /path/to/files/

Example: tar -cvf project.tar /home/user/project/
This creates an archive project.tar from the contents of the /home/user/project/ directory.

To extract the contents of a .tar archive:
tar -xvf archive.tar

tar with gzip

Create a compressed archive using gzip:
tar -czvf archive.tar.gz /path/to/files/

Example: tar -czvf project.tar.gz /home/user/project/
This creates a gzip-compressed project.tar.gz archive from the /home/user/project/ directory.

To extract a .tar.gz file:
tar -xzvf archive.tar.gz

tar with bzip2

Create a compressed archive using bzip2:
tar -cjvf archive.tar.bz2 /path/to/files/

Example:
tar -cjvf project.tar.bz2 /home/user/project/
This creates a bzip2-compressed project.tar.bz2 archive.

To extract a .tar.bz2 file:
tar -xjvf archive.tar.bz2

gzip

Compress a single file:
gzip filename.txt

Example: gzip report.txt
This compresses report.txt to report.txt.gz.

To decompress a .gz file:
gzip -d report.txt.gz

bzip2

Compress a single file (usually with higher compression than gzip):
bzip2 filename.txt

Example: bzip2 largefile.txt
This compresses largefile.txt to largefile.txt.bz2.

To decompress a .bz2 file:
bzip2 -d largefile.txt.bz2

zip

Create a .zip archive:
zip archive.zip file1.txt file2.txt

Example: zip project.zip *.txt
This compresses all .txt files in the current directory into project.zip.

To compress a directory and its contents:
zip -r archive.zip /path/to/directory

Example: zip -r backup.zip /home/user/documents/
This creates a .zip archive of the documents directory.

unzip

Extract the contents of a .zip archive:
unzip archive.zip

Example: unzip project.zip
This extracts all files from project.zip into the current directory.

Working with Symbolic and Hard Links

In Linux, symbolic (soft) and hard links are used to create references to files and directories. A symbolic link (created with the ln -s command) is like a shortcut or alias that points to the original file or directory. It can span across different file systems and can link to directories, but it relies on the original file's path, meaning it becomes broken if the target is moved or deleted. A hard link (created with the ln command without the -s option) directly references the inode of the original file, meaning it points to the same data on disk, essentially creating another name for the same file. Hard links cannot link to directories (except for the . and .. links that exist within directories) and must reside on the same file system. Both symbolic and hard links are valuable for file management, allowing multiple access points to the same data, which can help with backups, system administration, and efficient file storage.

ln - Symbolic Link (Soft Link)

A symbolic link is like a shortcut or alias to another file or directory. It can span across different file systems and points to the original file by name.

Create a symbolic link:
ln -s /path/to/original/file /path/to/link

Example:
ln -s /home/user/documents/report.txt /home/user/desktop/report_link.txt
This creates a symbolic link named report_link.txt in the dsk directory, pointing to the report.txt file in the docs directory.

Check if the symbolic link is working:
ls -l /home/user/dsk/report_link.txt

Output (example):
lrwxrwxrwx 1 user user 39 Mar 10 12:00 /home/user/dsk/report_link.txt -> /home/user/docs/report.txt

Remove a symbolic link:
rm /home/user/dsk/report_link.txt

ln - Hard Link
A hard link creates another directory entry for the same file, which means both the original file and the hard link point to the same inode on the disk. If one link is deleted, the data remains accessible through the other link.

Create a hard link:
ln /path/to/original/file /path/to/link

Example:
ln /home/user/docs/report.txt /home/user/dsk/report_hardlink.txt
This creates a hard link named report_hardlink.txt in the dsk directory, which points to the same data as report.txt.

Check the hard link:
ls -li /home/user/docs/report.txt /home/user/dsk/hardlink.txt

Output (example):
1234567 -rw-r--r-- 2 user user 1024 Mar 10 12:00 /home/user/docs/report.txt
1234567 -rw-r--r-- 2 user user 1024 Mar 10 12:00 /home/user/dsk/hardlink.txt

Both files show the same inode number (1234567), indicating they point to the same data on disk.

Remove a hard link:

rm /home/user/dsk/hardlink.txt

The original file (report.txt) remains intact since both the hard link and the original file point to the same data.

Chapter 3: Text Editors

Linux offers a variety of text editors, both command-line and graphical, to cater to different user needs. Command-line editors like Vim and Nano are highly popular for their efficiency in terminal-based environments. Vim, an advanced editor, provides powerful features like syntax highlighting, multi-file editing, and customizable key bindings, making it ideal for experienced users who prefer a fast, keyboard-centric workflow. Nano, on the other hand, is a simpler, more user-friendly option, perfect for beginners or quick edits with intuitive keyboard shortcuts.

One of the key advantages of using text editors in Linux is the ability to work with multiple files simultaneously. A user can open several terminal windows or use tmux or screen, terminal multiplexers that allow for the use of multiple "screens" in one terminal session. These tools enable users to split the terminal window into multiple panes, each running a different instance of a text editor. This means you can edit several text files at the same time, making it easier to work on related tasks or compare files side by side without having to constantly switch between windows or tabs.

For graphical environments, Gedit (often found in GNOME) and Kate (KDE's editor) provide a more traditional GUI experience, featuring support for syntax highlighting, search-and-replace functionality, and file management in a more visual setting. These editors are user-friendly and suitable for users who prefer a mouse-driven interface, offering the ability to easily switch between open files and use visual features for editing and navigation. Emacs, though often used in a command-line environment, also has a GUI version and is a versatile and highly extensible editor, favored by developers for its wide range of customizable features, from text editing to project management. For those looking for modern, cross-platform interfaces, Sublime Text and Visual Studio Code stand out with advanced features like code completion, version control, and plugin support. These editors are popular for web development and software engineering, supporting a wide range of programming languages and frameworks.

Additionally, users can take advantage of tmux or screen in a graphical terminal to work on multiple files simultaneously, making it easier to organize and switch between tasks. Each of these editors has its strengths and can be chosen based on user preferences, system resources, and the nature of the tasks at hand. Whether you need a lightweight editor like Gedit or a full-featured IDE like Visual Studio Code, the right editor can make a significant difference in productivity and workflow.

Introduction to Common Linux Text Editors

nano

Nano is a simple, user-friendly command-line text editor, making it an excellent choice for beginners. It provides an easy-to-understand interface with keyboard shortcuts displayed at the bottom.

Open a file:
nano filename.txt

Save the file:
Press Ctrl + O, then press Enter to confirm.

Exit the editor:
Press Ctrl + X. If you have unsaved changes, Nano will prompt you to save them before quitting.

vim/vi
Vim is an enhanced version of the older vi editor, known for its powerful features but with a steeper learning curve. Vim operates in multiple modes: normal mode, insert mode, and command mode.

Open a file:
vim filename.txt
or, if vi is used:
vi filename.txt

Switch to insert mode:
Press i to enter insert mode, where you can start typing text.

Save the file:
Press Esc to return to normal mode.
Type :w and press Enter to save the file.

Exit the editor:

Press Esc to ensure you're in normal mode.
Type :q and press Enter to quit. If there are unsaved changes, it will warn you.
If you want to quit without saving changes, type :q! and press Enter.
To save and quit simultaneously, type :wq and press Enter.

emacs

Emacs is a highly customizable and extensible text editor, favored by many developers for its extensive feature set. It can be complex for new users, but its flexibility makes it a powerful tool once mastered.

Open a file:
emacs filename.txt

Save the file:
Press Ctrl + X followed by Ctrl + S.

Exit the editor: Press Ctrl + X followed by Ctrl + C. If there are unsaved changes, Emacs will prompt you to save them before quitting.

Editing Configuration Files

Editing system configuration files in Linux is a critical task that requires caution to avoid causing system instability or security vulnerabilities. The best practice is to always back up configuration files before making any changes. This allows you to restore the file to its original state if something goes wrong. It's also advisable to use a text editor with elevated privileges, such as sudo nano or sudo vim, when editing system files to ensure that you have the necessary permissions. When making changes, it's important to edit one file at a time and to thoroughly understand the syntax and options in the configuration file to avoid misconfigurations. Commenting out lines instead of deleting them can provide a quick way to test changes and revert to the previous configuration if needed.

For major changes, it's wise to test the system after editing a configuration file to ensure that the new settings are working as expected without causing issues. Additionally, if working on a server or critical system, consider doing configuration changes during maintenance windows or in a test environment to minimize the impact of potential problems. Finally, always document the changes you make, so you or others can track the modifications and their rationale in the future. Following these best practices helps maintain system stability and security while allowing for effective configuration management.

Best practices for editing system config files safely

Back Up Configuration Files

Before making any changes to a configuration file, it is crucial to back it up. For example, if you want to edit the /etc/hosts file, you can back it up like this:

sudo cp /etc/hosts /etc/hosts.bak
This ensures that you have a copy to restore in case something goes wrong.

Using Elevated Privileges
To edit configuration files that require root access (such as network settings or user configurations), use sudo with a text editor like nano or vim.

For example, to edit the /etc/fstab file:
sudo nano /etc/fstab
or
sudo vim /etc/fstab

This ensures you have the necessary permissions to save the file after editing.

Commenting Out Lines Instead of Deleting
If you're testing changes in a configuration file, it's a good idea to comment out the lines you modify rather than deleting them, so you can quickly revert if needed. For example, in /etc/ssh/sshd_config:
Disable password authentication (test purpose)
PasswordAuthentication yes

By commenting out the line, you can safely test the change and undo it if necessary.

Editing One File at a Time
When configuring multiple services, avoid editing several configuration files simultaneously. Instead, focus on one file at a time, test your changes, and then move on to the next.

For example, if you're setting up a web server, first edit the Apache configuration:
sudo nano /etc/httpd/httpd.conf

Test the configuration using:
sudo apachectl configtest

Once you're confident it's working, then move on to other files, such as firewall rules or DNS configurations.

Test the System After Changes
After editing a system configuration file, always test to ensure the changes work as expected.

For example, after changing /etc/network/interfaces to configure a static IP:
sudo ifdown eth0 && sudo ifup eth0

Then check the network status:
ifconfig eth0

This confirms that the changes took effect without causing network issues.

Perform Changes During Maintenance Windows
If you're editing a configuration on a production server, perform changes during a scheduled maintenance window to minimize disruptions. For instance, make sure the system is not handling critical tasks like user logins or active transactions while you edit /etc/systemd/system/ to change a service configuration.

Document Your Changes

Always document what changes were made to the configuration files and why. You can add comments directly in the configuration file or keep an external changelog.

For example, in /etc/sudoers, add a comment before any modification:

Added user 'john' to allow sudo access
john ALL=(ALL) ALL

This helps keep track of your changes, which is essential for troubleshooting or audits later.

By following these steps, you ensure that your system configuration changes are safe, testable, and reversible, reducing the risk of errors or system downtime.

Edit multiple files using Linux Text Editors

Working with multiple files simultaneously is a common requirement when editing configuration or code files in Linux. Many text editors offer ways to open and edit multiple files at once, either within the same window or across separate windows, making it easier to manage different tasks concurrently.

Below are instructions for working with multiple files using popular text editors:

Vim (Vi Improved)

Vim is highly efficient for managing multiple files using its built-in capabilities. To work with multiple files in Vim:

Open multiple files: You can open several files at once by specifying them on the command line.

For example:
vim file1.txt file2.txt

This will open both files in tabs, and you can switch between them using :n (next) or :prev (previous).

Split the window: You can split the window into multiple panes to view and edit multiple files at once:
:vsp file2.txt # Vertically split the window
:sp file2.txt   # Horizontally split the window
Switch between panes using Ctrl-w w (to cycle through splits).

Edit files in buffers: Vim automatically opens each file in its own buffer, and you can navigate through them using :bnext (next buffer) and :bprev (previous buffer).

Nano

Nano is simpler and doesn't have as many features as Vim, but it still supports working with multiple files.

Open multiple files: To open multiple files, you can launch Nano with several filenames:

nano file1.txt file2.txt
You can switch between files using Ctrl-w (to search) and Ctrl-x (to exit). However, Nano is limited to editing one file at a time in the same window.

Open files in separate terminals: If you need to edit multiple files at once, you can open separate terminal windows or tabs, each running nano with a different file.

For example:
nano file1.txt

In another terminal window:
nano file2.txt

Emacs
Emacs is another powerful editor that excels at managing multiple files. It provides several ways to open and switch between files.

Open multiple files: You can open multiple files by specifying them on the command line:

emacs file1.txt file2.txt

Each file will open in a separate buffer, and you can switch between them with Ctrl-x b and typing the buffer name.

Split the window: You can split the window into multiple sections to view different files:

```
Ctrl-x 2  # Split window horizontally
Ctrl-x 3  # Split window vertically
```

After splitting, use Ctrl-x o to move between the splits. You can open different files in each split.

Edit files in buffers: Like Vim, Emacs also opens files in buffers, allowing you to cycle through them using Ctrl-x < (previous buffer) and Ctrl-x > (next buffer).

Graphical Editors

In graphical text editors like (Gedit, Kate, Sublime Text, Visual Studio Code), handling multiple files is straightforward with tabs and window management.

Open multiple files: Simply open each file in a new tab. For example, in Gedit:

```
gedit file1.txt file2.txt
```

This will open both files in separate tabs within the same window, and you can switch between them by clicking the tab or using keyboard shortcuts like Ctrl+Tab.

Drag-and-drop files: You can drag files from the file manager into the editor window to open them.

Split window (Sublime Text, Visual Studio Code): In editors like Sublime Text or VS Code, you can also split the editor window to view multiple files side by side. For example:

In Sublime Text: Use View > Layout to select how many panes you want.

In Visual Studio Code: Use View > Split Editor to split the editor vertically or horizontally.

General Tips for Working with Multiple Files

Terminal Multiplexers: If you're working in a terminal and need to manage multiple files, terminal multiplexers like tmux or screen can help you organize different terminals within one window. You can open multiple text editors in separate panes or windows and switch between them easily. For example, in tmux, you can create a new pane with Ctrl-b % (vertical split) or Ctrl-b " (horizontal split), then open different text editors in each pane.

Focus on One Task: When working with multiple files, try to focus on one task at a time (e.g., editing configuration files, writing code) to avoid confusion. Keep related files open together to streamline the editing process.

Search and Replace in Editors

Search and replace is a powerful feature in text editors that allows users to quickly locate and modify specific text within a file. In Nano, you can search with Ctrl-W and replace with Ctrl-\. In Vim, use / to search and :s/old/new/g to replace text, with options for replacing in specific lines or throughout the whole file. In Emacs, search with Ctrl-s and replace with M-%, which lets you confirm each change. These tools save time and effort when editing large files or making repetitive changes.

Nano

Search: Press Ctrl-W, then type the text you want to search for, such as error, and press Enter.

Replace: Press Ctrl-\, then type the search term (e.g., error), followed by the replacement text (e.g., mistake). Nano will ask if you want to replace each occurrence. Press Y to replace or N to skip.

Vim

Search: Press / and type the term you want to search for, e.g., /error, then press Enter. This will find the first occurrence of error.

Replace: To replace a word on the current line:
:s/error/mistake/g

This replaces all occurrences of error with mistake in the current line. To replace throughout the whole file, use:
:%s/error/mistake/g

You can also add c at the end to confirm each change, like:
:%s/error/mistake/gc

Emacs

Search: Press Ctrl-s and type the search term, e.g., error. Emacs will highlight the first match. Press Ctrl-s again to find the next occurrence.

Replace: Press M-% (Alt + Shift + %), then type the search term (e.g., error) and the replacement text (e.g., mistake). Emacs will prompt you to confirm each replacement with y to replace, n to skip, or ! to replace all occurrences without further prompts.

Chapter 4: User and Permission Management

Linux user and permission management is a fundamental aspect of system administration, ensuring that users have appropriate access to files, directories, and system resources. Each user in Linux is assigned a unique username and user ID (UID), and can be grouped into user groups for easier management of permissions. Permissions control who can read, write, or execute a file or directory, and are represented by a combination of owner, group, and others. The chmod command is used to change file permissions, while chown allows changing ownership, and chgrp modifies group ownership. Administrators can also use the usermod, useradd, and groupadd commands to manage users and groups. Additionally, the /etc/passwd file stores user information, and /etc/shadow contains encrypted password data. With proper user and permission management, Linux systems maintain security, restricting unauthorized access while allowing necessary interactions with system resources.

Managing Users and Groups

Managing users and groups in Linux is essential for system administration and security. The useradd command is used to create a new user, while usermod modifies user account settings, such as changing a username or adding the user to a different group. The passwd command is employed to set or change a user's password. For managing groups, groupadd creates new groups, and id displays user and group information, including UID, GID, and group memberships. The whoami command shows the currently logged-in user's username. Together, these tools enable administrators to efficiently manage user access and permissions, ensuring appropriate security and organization within a Linux system.

useradd - Create a new user:
sudo useradd john
This creates a user named "john."

Usermod – Modify an existing user
sudo usermod -aG sudo john
This adds the user "john" to the "sudo" group, granting administrative privileges.

passwd – Set or change a user's password
sudo passwd john
This prompts you to enter and confirm a new password for the user "john."

groupadd – Create a new group
sudo groupadd newbies

This creates a new group called "newbies."

id – Display user and group information

id john

This shows the user ID (UID), group ID (GID), and the groups that "john" belongs to.

whoami – Display logged-in user's username

whoami

This will output the username of the user currently logged in, such as john.

who or w: To see who is logged into the system

Example:

who

This will display the login name, terminal, login time, and from where the user is logged in.

w: The **w** command provides more detailed information about the users logged in, their activity, and system usage.

Example:

w

This will show not only who is logged in but also their current processes and idle times.

tty1: Refers to a terminal (usually a physical or virtual console). You might use this when checking a specific terminal session. For example, if you type who or w while logged into tty1, you'll see details of who is logged into that terminal.

If you run **who tty1**, it would show you the user logged into that specific terminal.

groups – Show the groups a user belongs to
groups john
This shows all the groups that the user "john" is a member of.

File and Directory Permissions

In Linux, file and directory permissions are crucial for controlling access and security. The chmod command modifies file permissions by setting read, write, and execute rights for the owner, group, and others. For example, chmod 755 file.txt grants read, write, and execute permissions to the owner, and read and execute permissions to the group and others.

The chown command changes the owner and/or group of a

file or directory, such as chown user:group file.txt. The chgrp command specifically modifies the group ownership, for instance, chgrp developers file.txt. umask sets the default permissions for newly created files and directories, ensuring that files are not given overly permissive rights by default. For more fine-grained control, setfacl allows setting Access Control Lists (ACLs), enabling specific permissions for individual users or groups beyond traditional owner/group/other categories, like setfacl -m u:john:r—file.txt to give the user "john" read-only access. These tools work together to manage file access, security, and collaboration in a multi-user environment.

Permission Types & Numeric Values

Each permission type is represented by a number:

Read (r) = 4

Write (w) = 2

Execute (x) = 1

The numeric value for each user category (owner, group, others) is the sum of these values based on the permissions granted.

Breakdown of the chmod Number

The chmod command uses a 3-digit or 4-digit number to specify the permissions for Owner, Group, and Others (and sometimes Special permissions like SetUID, SetGID, and Sticky bit).

Here's how it works:

Example: chmod 755 file.txt

The first digit (7) represents the owner permissions.
The second digit (5) represents the group permissions.
The third digit (5) represents the others permissions.

Breakdown:

Owner (7): 4 (read) + 2 (write) + 1 (execute) = 7 → rwx (read, write, execute)

Group (5): 4 (read) + 1 (execute) = 5 → r-x (read, execute)

Others (5): 4 (read) + 1 (execute) = 5 → r-x (read, execute)

So, chmod 755 gives the owner full permissions (read, write, execute), while group and others get read and execute permissions.

Common chmod Numbers

777: rwxrwxrwx (Owner, Group, Others have full permissions)

755: rwxr-xr-x (Owner has full permissions, Group and Others have read and execute permissions)

644: rw-r--r-- (Owner can read and write, Group and Others can only read)

700: rwx------ (Owner has full permissions, Group and Others have no permissions)

600: rw------- (Owner can read and write, Group and Others have no permissions)

Special Permissions:

SetUID (4): Makes a program run as the owner.

SetGID (2): Makes a program run as the group.

Sticky Bit (1): Restricts file deletion in shared directories (only the owner can delete their files).

Example with special permissions: chmod 1777 /tmp
The 1 (Sticky bit) combined with 777 gives rwxrwxrwt, which means full permissions for everyone but with restrictions on file deletion in the /tmp directory.

By using numeric values, you can efficiently modify file and directory permissions based on what you need for your environment.

Example Usage of File and Directory Commands

chmod – Change file permissions

Example 1: Set the file permissions of file.txt to rwxr-xr-x (read, write, execute for the owner, and read, execute for the group and others):
chmod 755 file.txt

Example 2: Remove write permission for the group and others:
chmod go-w file.txt

chown – Change file owner and/or group

Example 1: Change the owner of file.txt to user "john" and the group to "admins":
chown john:admins file.txt

Example 2: Change only the owner of file.txt to user "alice":
chown alice file.txt

chgrp – Change file group

Example 1: Change the group of file.txt to "newbies":
chgrp newbies file.txt

Example 2: Change the group of all .txt files in the current directory to "writers":
chgrp writers *.txt

umask – Set default file creation permissions

Example 1: Set the default umask to 022 (files created will have 755 permissions, directories will have 755 by default):
umask 022

Example 2: Temporarily set the umask to 0777 for more restrictive file permissions (all new files will have no permissions for group and others):
umask 0777

setfacl – Set Access Control List (ACL)
Used for more detailed permisions

Example 1: Grant read-only permission to user "john" on file.txt:

```
setfacl -m u:john:r-- file.txt
```

Example 2: Remove any ACL entries for user "john" on file.txt:
```
setfacl -x u:john file.txt
```

Switching Users

In Linux, switching users can be accomplished using the su and sudo commands. The su (substitute user) command allows a user to switch to another user account, typically the root account, by typing su followed by the username. For example, su - root switches to the root user. The sudo (superuser do) command allows authorized users to run specific commands as the root user or another user, providing more controlled access to administrative privileges.

For example, sudo apt-get update lets a regular user run the update command with root privileges. Regular users have limited permissions but can perform certain administrative tasks with sudo if granted the necessary permissions by the system administrator, typically configured in the /etc/sudoers file.

su (Substitute User):

To switch to the root user:
```
su -
```

This will prompt for the root password. The - ensures that you get the root user's environment.

To switch to a specific user (e.g., username):
su - username
This will prompt for the password of the user you're switching to.

sudo (Superuser Do):

To run a command with root privileges:
sudo command

For example, to update package lists:
sudo apt-get update
You will need to enter your user password, assuming your user is authorized to run sudo commands.

Switching to Another User Using sudo (if configured):
To run a command as another user (e.g., username), use:
sudo -u username command

For example, to list files as another user:
sudo -u username ls

Chapter 5: Shell Management and Multi-Shell Navigation

Shell management and multi-shell navigation in Linux involve using multiple terminal sessions to manage different tasks simultaneously. The shell acts as the command-line interface for interacting with the operating system, and users can open multiple shell instances to run commands in parallel or work on different files and processes. Tools like tmux and screen enable users to create multiple virtual terminal windows within a single terminal session, allowing for efficient multitasking and easy switching between tasks. By using these tools, users can split their terminal window into multiple panes, each running its own shell, or detach and resume sessions, making it easier to work on several tasks without losing progress. Additionally, commands like bash, zsh, and fish are popular shells that can be customized for various workflows, making multi-shell navigation a powerful technique for advanced users.

Opening New Shells

In Linux, users can open new sessions by switching between different TTYs (teletype terminals) using the key combinations Ctrl+Alt+F1 to Ctrl+Alt+F6. These key combinations allow users to access up to six different virtual consoles or terminal sessions, where each TTY can run a separate instance of the shell. This is particularly useful for multitasking, troubleshooting, or managing multiple processes without the need for a graphical interface. For example, Ctrl+Alt+F1 brings up the first TTY, Ctrl+Alt+F2 opens the second, and so on. The graphical user interface (GUI) typically runs on Ctrl+Alt+F7 (or later, depending on the system), so users can easily switch back and forth between the GUI and text-based terminals. To switch back to a specific TTY, simply use the appropriate key combination, allowing users to work across multiple sessions seamlessly.

Example Steps – Open New Shell

Switch to TTY1:
Press **Ctrl+Alt+F1**. This will take you to the first virtual terminal. If you're logged into the system, you should see a login prompt where you can enter your username and password.

Switch to TTY2:
Press **Ctrl+Alt+F2**. This will open a new terminal session where you can log in again or perform other tasks independently of TTY1.

Switch to TTY3:
Press **Ctrl+Alt+F3**. This switches you to the third virtual console, providing yet another clean session for different tasks.

Work on each terminal:

You can now use each TTY independently, such as running different processes, editing files, or performing administrative tasks in parallel.

For instance, you could be running a web server on **TTY1**, editing a script on **TTY2**, and monitoring system resources on **TTY3**.

Switch back to the graphical session:
Press **Ctrl+Alt+F7** (or **Ctrl+Alt+F1**, depending on the Linux distribution) to return to the graphical user interface (GUI), where you can continue working with desktop applications. By switching between these TTYs, you can manage multiple tasks efficiently without needing multiple graphical windows, and the system remains responsive.

Launching New Shells

Launching new shells in a Linux session allows users to work with different shell environments within the same terminal window. By default, most Linux distributions use bash (Bourne Again Shell), but users can switch to other shells like zsh (Z Shell), fish (Friendly Interactive Shell), or others, depending on their preferences or the task at hand. To launch a new shell, simply type the name of the desired shell, such as bash, zsh, or fish, and press Enter. For example, typing zsh will start the Z Shell in the current terminal session. If you want to switch back to the default shell, you can type exit to return to the previous shell or open a new one. This flexibility allows users to experiment with different shell features, customize their environment, or run specialized commands, all within a single session.

Example Steps – Launch New Shells

Open a terminal (if not already open).

Start a new bash shell:
If you are already using a different shell (for example, zsh or fish), you can switch to the bash shell by typing:
bash
This will launch a new instance of the bash shell. You can tell you're in a new shell by the prompt changing (if customized) or simply by the environment you're in.

Start a zsh shell:

To switch to the zsh shell, type:
zsh

This will open the zsh shell in the current terminal. You'll see the prompt change to the default zsh prompt, or your custom prompt if you've configured zsh.

Start a fish shell:

Similarly, to start the fish shell, type:
fish

This will start the fish shell, which has a more user-friendly and colorful interface compared to bash or zsh.

Exit and return to the previous shell:
If you want to return to the previous shell (for example, back to bash or zsh), you can type:
exit

This will close the current shell session and bring you back to the previous one.

Example:
zsh
% echo "Now you're in Z Shell"
Now you're in Z Shell
% exit
bash
echo "Back to Bash"
Back to Bash

In this example:
The user switched from bash to zsh and then returned back to bash using the exit command.

Creating Subshells

Creating subshells in Linux allows users to spawn new shell instances within the current shell session, providing an isolated environment for running commands without affecting the parent shell. This is commonly done by invoking bash within an existing shell, which opens a new subshell. For example, typing bash inside a running terminal will open a new instance of the Bash shell, where the user can execute commands independently. Any environment changes, such as setting variables or altering directories, will only affect the subshell. To exit the subshell and return to the parent shell, simply type exit. Subshells are useful for testing commands or running scripts without altering the main environment, and they provide a flexible way to manage different tasks concurrently.

Example Steps - Create subshells

Open a terminal:
If you're already in a terminal, you'll likely be in the default shell (often bash).

Launch a subshell using bash:
Type bash and press Enter. This opens a new instance of the Bash shell, which is a subshell of the current one.
bash
You should notice the prompt changes, indicating you are now in a subshell (the prompt may change depending on your shell configuration).

Make changes in the subshell:
For example, you can set an environment variable in the subshell.
MY_VAR="Hello from the subshell"
echo $MY_VAR
Hello from the subshell
This variable is set only within the subshell and won't affect the parent shell.

Exit the subshell and return to the parent shell:
When you're done with the subshell, type exit to close it and return to the original shell.
exit
echo $MY_VAR
(No output, as MY_VAR was only set in the subshell)

Breakdown:
When you run bash inside the shell, it creates a subshell.
Any changes (like setting variables or navigating directories) are local to that subshell.

After typing exit, you return to the original shell, and the changes made in the subshell are discarded.
This demonstrates how subshells can be used to isolate tasks and keep the main shell environment unchanged.

Terminal Multiplexers

Terminal multiplexers like tmux and screen are powerful tools for managing multiple terminal sessions within a single window. These utilities allow users to run, monitor, and switch between multiple sessions, or "windows," within one terminal, without the need to open several separate terminal instances. tmux and screen both offer features such as session persistence (allowing sessions to continue running even after disconnecting), window splitting, and easy session navigation. For instance, with tmux, you can split your terminal into multiple panes to run different tasks simultaneously, and switch between them using keyboard shortcuts. Similarly, screen provides the ability to create and manage multiple windows, detach and reattach to sessions, and even share sessions with other users. Both tools enhance productivity and multitasking by allowing users to efficiently manage and monitor several processes in parallel from a single terminal interface.

Backgrounding and Foregrounding

Backgrounding and foregrounding are techniques used to manage processes in a Linux terminal. When a process is running in the foreground, it occupies the terminal, meaning you cannot use the terminal for other tasks until the process completes. To free up the terminal without terminating the process, you can pause it using Ctrl+Z, which suspends the process and moves it to the background. Once in the background, the process continues running, and you can use the terminal for other commands. You can bring the background process back to the foreground using the fg command, allowing it to resume and occupy the terminal. Alternatively, the bg command can be used to keep a process running in the background, freeing the terminal for other tasks while the process continues in the background. This allows for efficient multitasking within the terminal environment.

Example Steps – Backgrounding & Foregrounding

Start a long-running command:
For example, let's start the sleep command, which pauses for a specified time (e.g., 10 seconds).
sleep 10

Pause the process using Ctrl+Z:
While the sleep command is running, press Ctrl+Z to pause (or suspend) the process. This sends the process into the background and stops it temporarily.

You'll see a message like:
[1]+ 12345 suspended sleep 10

View the suspended jobs:

To list the background jobs, use the jobs command:
jobs
This will show something like:
[1]+ 12345 suspended sleep 10

Bring the process to the foreground using fg:
To bring the paused process back to the foreground (to resume its execution), use the fg command:
fg %1

This will bring job number 1 (the sleep command) back into the foreground and continue execution. If you had more jobs, you could replace %1 with the appropriate job number.

Send the process to the background using bg:

Alternatively, you can send the suspended job to the background to allow it to continue running without blocking the terminal:
bg %1

This will resume the sleep 10 command in the background, and you can continue using the terminal for other tasks while it finishes.

Summary of Commands:

Ctrl+Z: Pauses the process and sends it to the background.

jobs: Lists background jobs.

fg %1: Brings job number 1 to the foreground.
bg %1: Continues job number 1 in the background.

This workflow is useful for managing long-running processes without locking up your terminal, allowing you to multitask efficiently.

Chapter 6: Process Management

Process management in Linux refers to the system's ability to handle running programs, or processes, and control their execution, resource allocation, and interaction with the system. Each process in Linux is identified by a unique Process ID (PID) and can be monitored, controlled, or terminated by the user or system. Common process management commands include ps (to view the list of running processes), top (for a real-time overview of system activity), and kill (to send signals to processes, typically to terminate them). Users can also control the priority of processes using nice and renice, or use nohup to run processes in the background, immune to hangups. Additionally, tools like htop provide an interactive interface for more advanced process management, making it easier to manage resources and troubleshoot system performance. Effective process management is essential for maintaining system stability and ensuring efficient use of computing resources.

Viewing and Managing Processes

Viewing and managing processes in Linux can be efficiently done using several tools like ps, top, htop, pgrep, and pkill. The ps command provides a snapshot of current processes, displaying information like PID, CPU usage, and running time, while top offers a dynamic, real-time view of system processes, updating regularly to show resource usage. For a more interactive and user-friendly experience, htop enhances top with additional features like color coding and easy navigation, allowing users to monitor and manage processes with more control. pgrep is useful for searching for processes based on their name or other attributes, making it easy to identify processes without scrolling through the entire list. Once identified, pkill allows users to terminate processes by name or other criteria, offering a convenient way to manage runaway or unnecessary tasks. Together, these tools provide comprehensive options for managing processes, improving both system performance and user control.

ps (Process Status)
The ps command displays a snapshot of current processes.

Basic usage - Show all running processes:
ps aux
a shows processes for all users.
u displays user-oriented output.
x includes processes not attached to a terminal.

Specific user processes: Show processes for a particular user:
ps -u username

top (Task Manager)
The top command provides real-time, dynamic monitoring of system processes.

Basic usage - Display live processes with CPU and memory usage:
top
You can press q to exit top.

Sorting by CPU usage: Press P in **top** to sort processes by CPU usage.

Sorting by memory usage: Press M in **top** to sort processes by memory usage.

htop (Interactive Task Manager)
htop is an enhanced version of top that is more user-friendly.

Basic usage: Show interactive process list:
htop
Use the arrow keys to scroll through the list.
Press F9 to kill a process.
Press q to quit htop.

pgrep (Process Grep)
The pgrep command searches for processes by name or other attributes.

Find process by name: Find the PID of a process (e.g., apache2):
pgrep apache2
This will return the PID of all apache2 processes running.

Find process by name and display full details: Use pgrep with **-l** for detailed output:
pgrep -l apache2

pkill (Process Kill by Name)

The pkill command allows you to terminate processes by name or other attributes.

Kill process by name: Terminate all processes with the name apache2:
pkill apache2
This will terminate all running instances of apache2.

Kill process by signal: Send a different signal (e.g., SIGTERM) to a process:
pkill -SIGTERM apache2

Killing Processes

In Linux, managing processes often involves terminating or "killing" processes that are no longer needed or are causing issues. The kill command is used to send signals to processes, with the default signal being SIGTERM (terminate), which politely asks a process to stop. It is typically used with a process ID (PID) to target a specific process.

Example Steps – Killing Processes

kill 1234
Where 1234 is the PID of the process. If a process does not respond to SIGTERM, a stronger signal like SIGKILL can be used with the -9 option:
kill -9 1234

The killall command allows you to terminate processes by name rather than by PID. For example, to kill all processes named firefox:
killall firefox

xkill provides a graphical way to kill a process by clicking on its window. When executed, it changes the mouse cursor to a cross, and clicking on any open window will immediately kill its associated process:
xkill

Scheduling Jobs

Scheduling jobs in Linux allows users to automate tasks and manage background processes efficiently. cron is a time-based job scheduler that runs commands or scripts at specific intervals, defined by the crontab file. Each user can set their own scheduled tasks using crontab -e, specifying the timing (minutes, hours, days) and the command to execute. For one-time scheduled tasks, the at command can be used, allowing jobs to run at a specific time in the future without the need for repetition. Meanwhile, jobs is used to list currently running background processes within a shell session, while bg sends a paused job (suspended with Ctrl+Z) to run in the background, and fg brings it back to the foreground. These commands provide flexibility in both scheduled and immediate task management, ensuring efficient use of system resources.

cron and crontab (Scheduling Recurring Jobs)

To schedule recurring tasks, you first need to edit the crontab for your user:
crontab -e

Inside the crontab file, you define jobs using the format:
minute hour day-of-month month day-of-week command

For example, to run a backup script every day at 2:30 AM:
30 2 * * * /path/to/backup.sh

To view current scheduled jobs for the user:
crontab -l

at (Scheduling One-Time Jobs)
The at command is used to schedule a one-time job.

For example, to schedule a system shutdown at 11 PM:
echo "sudo shutdown -h now" | at 23:00

You can list all scheduled at jobs with:

Atq

jobs (List Background Jobs)

The jobs command lists jobs that are running or paused in the background within your current shell session. After starting a background task, you can check its status:
Jobs

bg (Run a Job in the Background)
If a task has been paused with Ctrl+Z, you can send it to run in the background using bg.

For example:
bg %1

This sends job 1 (from the jobs list) to the background.

fg (Bring a Job to the Foreground)
If a job is running in the background, you can bring it back to the foreground using fg.

For example:
fg %1

This brings job 1 (from the jobs list) back to the foreground.

Example Workflow

Start a command, then suspend it with Ctrl+Z:
ping google.com
[Ctrl+Z]

Move the job to the background:
bg

View all jobs:
jobs

Bring the job back to the foreground:
 Fg

Process Prioritization

Process prioritization in Linux allows users to control how much CPU time a process gets relative to others by adjusting its "niceness." The nice command is used to start a process with a specified priority, where a higher niceness value means the process will be less prioritized compared to others.

For example, running a backup script with a low priority can be done with:

nice -n 10 /path/to/backup.sh

The renice command changes the priority of an already running process.

You can lower a process's priority (or make it "nicer") by specifying its process ID (PID) like so:
renice 15 1234

Here, 1234 is the PID of the running process. Prioritizing processes helps manage system resources effectively, ensuring that critical tasks get the necessary CPU time while lower-priority processes run in the background.

nice (Starting a Process with a Specific Priority)

By default, processes are started with a niceness of 0. To start a process with a lower priority (i.e., with a higher niceness value), use the nice command.

Example: Run a backup script with a niceness value of 10, making it a lower priority task:
nice -n 10 /path/to/backup.sh

This starts the backup.sh script with less CPU priority compared to other processes.

renice (Changing the Priority of a Running Process)

If you have a process that is already running and you want to change its niceness, you can use renice. You'll need the Process ID (PID) of the process, which you can find using the ps or top commands.

Example: Change the niceness of a running process with PID 1234 to 15 (lower priority):
renice 15 1234

This command reduces the CPU priority of the process with PID 1234, allowing other processes to take precedence.

Workflow Example (nice & renice)

Start a CPU-intensive process like dd (which copies data) with normal priority:
dd if=/dev/zero of=/dev/null &

Use ps to find the PID of the dd process:
ps aux | grep dd

Change its niceness to reduce its CPU priority:
renice 10 1234
(Assuming 1234 is the PID of the dd process.)

These commands allow you to control system resource allocation, ensuring that critical tasks get enough CPU time, while less important tasks run with lower priority.

Chapter 7: System Monitoring and Performance

System monitoring and performance management in Linux involve using various tools to observe system activity, resource usage, and overall health. Tools like top and htop provide real-time data on CPU, memory, and process usage, allowing users to identify resource-intensive processes and take action. The vmstat command offers a detailed view of system performance metrics such as memory, swap, and disk I/O. Additionally, iostat and sar help monitor disk activity and overall system performance over time. Regular monitoring ensures that resources are efficiently allocated, bottlenecks are identified, and performance is optimized for smooth system operations.

System Resource Monitoring

System resource monitoring in Linux is crucial for assessing the overall health and performance of the system. The free command displays available and used memory, helping monitor RAM usage. To check disk space usage, df provides an overview of file system capacity, while du breaks down space usage by directories or files. vmstat reports on system processes, memory, paging, and I/O, offering insights into system performance. iostat focuses on disk I/O statistics, and sar gathers system activity data over time for more detailed performance analysis. Finally, uptime provides a quick view of system load averages and how long the system has been running. These tools collectively offer a comprehensive way to monitor system resources and ensure efficient performance management.

free (Displays memory usage)

free -h

This command shows the available, used, and free memory in a human-readable format (-h).

df (Displays disk space usage)

df -h

This provides an overview of your file system's disk usage, showing available and used space in human-readable format.

du (Shows disk usage for directories and files)

du -sh /home/user/

This will show the total size of the /home/user/ directory in a summarized human-readable format (-sh).

vmstat (Reports virtual memory and system activity)

vmstat 5

This command provides system performance data every 5 seconds, including information about processes, memory, paging, and CPU usage.

iostat (Monitors CPU and disk I/O)

iostat

This displays CPU statistics and input/output statistics for devices and partitions.

sar (Collects and reports system activity)

sar -u 5

This command displays CPU usage (-u) every 5 seconds, helping to track system performance over time.

uptime (Shows system uptime and load averages)

uptime

This command shows how long the system has been running, the number of users, and the load average over 1, 5, and 15 minutes.

cal (Display a calendar in the terminal)
By default, it shows the current month's calendar, but you can also view specific months or years, as well as customize the output.

Display the current month's calendar:
cal

This shows the calendar for the current month.

Display a specific month and year:
cal 12 2024

This displays the calendar for December 2024.

Display a full year calendar:
cal 2024

This shows the calendar for the entire year 2024.

Highlight the current day:
cal -h

This highlights the current day in the calendar.

Display a Julian calendar (days numbered 1 through 365):

cal -j

This shows the current month with Julian day numbers.

Disk Usage and Space

Managing disk usage and space in Linux is essential for ensuring system performance and avoiding full disks. The df command provides an overview of disk space usage across all mounted file systems, showing how much space is used and available. For more granular analysis, du is used to examine the disk usage of specific directories or files, helping to identify large files consuming space. lsblk lists information about block devices such as hard drives, including partitions and their mount points. Finally, fdisk is a utility used for managing disk partitions, allowing users to create, modify, or delete partitions. These tools together offer comprehensive control over disk space and usage.

df (Show disk space usage of mounted file systems)

df -h

This command displays disk usage in human-readable format (MB, GB), showing the available and used space for each mounted file system.

du (Shows disk usage of directories or files)

du -sh /var/log

This command shows the total disk space used by the /var/log directory, displayed in a human-readable summarized format.

lsblk (Lists information about block devices)

lsblk

This command shows all block devices like hard drives, their partitions, sizes, and mount points.

fdisk (Manage disk partitions)

sudo fdisk -l

This command lists the details of all partitions on your disks, including sizes and partition types.

Monitoring Logs

Monitoring system logs is essential for troubleshooting and maintaining Linux systems. The tail -f command allows users to monitor logs in real-time by displaying the most recent entries in a log file and updating the output as new lines are added. For more advanced logging, journalctl is used to query and display logs from the systemd journal, offering more powerful filtering options, including time-based queries and logs for specific services. System logs are typically stored in the /var/log/ directory, where administrators can find important log files like syslog, auth.log, and dmesg. Regular monitoring of logs helps detect issues such as system errors, security breaches, and hardware failures, allowing for prompt resolutions.

tail -f (Monitor the end of a log file in real-time)

tail -f /var/log/syslog

This command will display the last few lines of the syslog file and keep updating the output as new log entries are added.

journalctl (View logs from the systemd journal)

journalctl -u apache2

This command displays logs related to the apache2 service. You can replace apache2 with any other service name to view its logs.

To view logs from the last boot:
journalctl -b

To follow logs in real-time for a service:
journalctl -u apache2 -f

Check logs in the /var/log/ directory: To list the logs in the /var/log/ directory:
ls /var/log/

To view a specific log file like auth.log (authentication logs):
cat /var/log/auth.log

You can use less or more to scroll through long log files:
less /var/log/dmesg

System Load and Performance

System load and performance monitoring are critical for maintaining the health and efficiency of a Linux system. System load refers to the amount of computational work the system is performing, and it is typically represented by the load average, which shows the number of processes in the system's run queue over a period of time (1, 5, and 15 minutes).

Tools like top and htop provide real-time monitoring of system resources, displaying CPU usage, memory usage, disk I/O, and process activity, helping users identify bottlenecks or resource-heavy processes. The uptime command gives a quick view of system load averages along with the system's runtime since the last boot. Additionally, the vmstat and iostat commands offer insights into virtual memory usage and I/O performance, respectively. Regularly monitoring system load and performance ensures that the system runs optimally and helps administrators address any issues before they impact system stability.

Load Average

Load average is a critical metric for understanding the overall health and performance of a Linux system. It indicates the number of processes that are either actively executing or waiting for CPU time, averaged over three different time intervals (1, 5, and 15 minutes). The uptime command provides a quick summary of the system's load averages, along with the system's uptime. For more detailed monitoring, top and htop are commonly used tools. top displays real-time statistics about processes, CPU usage, memory consumption, and load averages, while htop offers a more user-friendly, interactive interface with color-coded outputs and the ability to filter or kill processes. By regularly checking the system load, administrators can identify performance issues, such as excessive CPU usage or resource contention, and take corrective actions to optimize system performance.

uptime (View system load averages and uptime)

uptime

Example output:
14:25:32 up 12 days, 3:21, 1 user, load average: 0.35, 0.45, 0.38
This command shows the current time, system uptime, number of logged-in users, and the load averages over 1, 5, and 15 minutes.

top (Real-time process monitoring, load averages)

top

Example output (the load averages are shown at the top of the screen):
top - 14:26:00 up 12 days, 3:22, 1 user, load average: 0.35, 0.45, 0.38
Tasks: 233 total, 1 running, 232 sleeping, 0 stopped, 0 zombie
%Cpu(s): 10.3 us, 3.5 sy, 0.0 ni, 86.1 id, 0.1 wa, 0.0 hi, 0.0 si, 0.0 st

htop (Interactive and colorful process monitoring)

htop

Example output (load averages are displayed at the top left corner of the screen):
Load average: 0.35, 0.45, 0.38

htop offers an interactive interface where you can scroll, search, and manage processes. The load averages are displayed alongside CPU, memory, and swap usage metrics.

CPU and Memory Usage

Monitoring and managing CPU and memory usage is essential for maintaining system performance and efficiency. Tools like vmstat, mpstat, and free are commonly used for this purpose. vmstat provides an overview of virtual memory statistics, including information on processes, memory, paging, block IO, traps, and CPU activity, allowing you to assess the overall system performance. mpstat, part of the sysstat package, provides detailed CPU usage statistics for individual processors, helping users identify CPU-bound processes or bottlenecks in multi-core systems. free gives a simple snapshot of memory usage, displaying the total, used, free, shared, and buffered memory, as well as swap usage. By regularly using these tools, administrators can ensure that memory and CPU resources are optimally allocated and can address performance issues before they lead to system slowdowns or failures.

vmstat (Virtual memory statistics)

vmstat

Example output:

```
procs -----------memory---------- ---swap-- -----io---- --system-- ----cpu----
 r  b  swpd  free  buff cache  si  so  bi  bo   in  cs us sy id wa st
 1 0    0 102356 32768 983212   0   0   1   4   75  62 3 2 95 0 0
```

This command displays memory usage, swap usage, I/O statistics, and CPU activity, which helps in diagnosing system performance issues.

mpstat (CPU usage statistics, per processor)

mpstat -P ALL

Example output:

CPU	%usr	%sys	%idle	%iowait	%irq	%soft
all	12.44	6.10	79.17	1.83	0.01	0.01
0	15.37	4.23	78.91	1.42	0.01	0.00
1	10.35	7.97	80.28	2.40	0.01	0.02

This command shows CPU usage statistics for each processor on the system, helping you identify if a specific core is under heavy load.

free (Memory usage statistics)

free -h

Example output:

	total	used	free	shared	buff/cache	available
Mem:	7.8Gi	1.2Gi	5.9Gi	168Mi	0.7Gi	6.3Gi

Swap: 2.0Gi   0B   2.0Gi

The free command shows total, used, and free memory, along with swap memory usage. The -h flag shows the values in human-readable format (e.g., GiB).

Disk and I/O Monitoring: Monitoring disk I/O

Disk and I/O monitoring is essential for assessing the performance and health of a system's storage. iostat is a powerful tool for reporting on CPU and input/output statistics, providing insights into disk activity. It can show read and write operations, as well as I/O wait times, helping identify bottlenecks in disk performance. For real-time monitoring, iotop allows you to observe disk I/O activity by showing which processes are consuming the most I/O resources. It is especially useful for detecting processes with high disk usage that may be slowing down the system. Both tools are critical for troubleshooting disk-related performance issues and ensuring optimal disk operations in Linux systems.

iostat - Input/Output Statistics

A command-line tool used to monitor system input/output device performance, including disk I/O statistics, CPU usage, and other system-related I/O metrics. iostat helps in tracking the performance of storage devices and identifying potential bottlenecks related to disk or CPU usage, which is crucial for system administrators to ensure optimal performance of their systems.

iostat -x 1

This shows extended statistics for all devices every 1 second.

iotop - I/O Top

A command-line utility that shows real-time information about processes that are performing I/O (input/output) operations, such as disk reads and writes. iotop is similar to top, but specifically focuses on displaying processes with the highest disk activity, making it useful for monitoring disk usage and identifying processes that may be causing performance bottlenecks due to excessive disk I/O.

sudo iotop

This command provides a real-time view of processes using the most disk I/O resources, requiring root privileges for access.

Network Monitoring

Network monitoring is a crucial part of system administration, allowing you to observe and analyze network connections, interfaces, and traffic. netstat is a classic tool for displaying network connections, routing tables, and interface statistics, providing insights into open ports and active connections. ss is a faster, more modern alternative to netstat, capable of displaying socket statistics, including listening ports and established connections, with more detailed output. ifstat allows you to monitor network interface statistics, showing real-time data transfer rates on each network interface. For a more graphical approach, nload provides a real-time, visual representation of incoming and outgoing network traffic on selected interfaces, making it easier to identify bandwidth usage and potential bottlenecks. These tools together offer comprehensive views of your system's network health and performance.

netstat - Network Statistics

A command-line tool used for displaying various network-related information, including active connections, routing tables, interface statistics, and more. It's commonly used for troubleshooting and monitoring network performance on both Linux and other operating systems.

netstat -tuln

This displays all listening ports (TCP and UDP) along with the corresponding IP addresses.

ss - Socket Statictics

A utility used to display detailed information about network sockets on a Linux system. ss is often considered a faster and more efficient alternative to netstat for showing information about established connections, listening ports, and socket statistics, especially when dealing with a large number of network connections.

ss -tuln

This is similar to netstat but with faster and more detailed output.

ifstat - Interface Statistics

A command-line tool used to display network interface statistics, showing real-time data such as the amount of incoming and outgoing traffic on network interfaces like Ethernet (eth0), Wi-Fi (wlan0), or others. ifstat is typically used for monitoring network throughput and diagnosing potential network performance issues.

ifstat

This shows real-time statistics for network interfaces such as eth0 or wlan0.

nload - Network Load

A command-line tool used to monitor network traffic in real-time. nload provides a visual representation of incoming and outgoing traffic on network interfaces, allowing users to observe bandwidth usage and network load in a graphical, text-based format. It's particularly useful for diagnosing network performance and monitoring network activity over time.

sudo nload

This provides a real-time graph of incoming and outgoing network traffic.

Chapter 8: Networking Essentials

Networking essentials for Linux involve understanding the basic tools and configurations that allow a Linux system to communicate over a network. Key components include configuring network interfaces using files like /etc/network/interfaces or using Netplan on newer distributions. The ip command is a powerful tool for managing network interfaces, routing, and IP addresses, replacing older tools like ifconfig. Additionally, the hostname command helps configure the system's network name, while /etc/hosts maps hostnames to IP addresses.

Tools like ping, traceroute, and netstat are used for troubleshooting and diagnosing network connectivity issues. Understanding firewalls, such as iptables or firewalld, is essential for securing network traffic. Finally, the Domain Name System (DNS) and configuring /etc/resolv.conf for DNS resolution are crucial for proper name-to-IP address mapping on the network. These essentials form the foundation for managing and troubleshooting networking on Linux systems.

Network Configuration

Network configuration in Linux is managed using several essential commands that control interfaces, routing, and system settings. The ifconfig command, though older and being phased out, is still used to display and configure network interfaces, such as ifconfig eth0 up to bring up the eth0 interface.

The more modern ip command is preferred for managing network settings; ip addr shows IP addresses assigned to interfaces, for example, ip addr show eth0, while ip link manages interface status, such as ip link set eth0 up to enable the interface. For managing routing tables, the route command is used, with route -n displaying the current routing table, and sudo route add default gw 192.168.1.1 adding a default gateway. The hostname command allows you to view or change the system's hostname, such as hostname myserver to set the system name.

On systems using NetworkManager, nmcli is a powerful command-line tool for managing network connections, with commands like nmcli dev status to check device status or nmcli con up <connection_name> to activate a network connection. These tools are fundamental for configuring and troubleshooting network settings on Linux systems.

ifconfig

View active network interfaces:
ifconfig

Bring up a network interface (e.g., eth0):
sudo ifconfig eth0 up

Assign an IP address to an interface (e.g., eth0):
sudo ifconfig eth0 192.168.1.10 netmask 255.255.255.0

ip addr

View IP addresses assigned to interfaces:
ip addr show

Assign an IP address to an interface (e.g., eth0):
sudo ip addr add 192.168.1.10/24 dev eth0

ip link

View network interface status:
ip link show

Bring up an interface (e.g., eth0):
sudo ip link set eth0 up

Bring down an interface (e.g., eth0):
sudo ip link set eth0 down

route

View the current routing table:

route -n

Add a default gateway:
sudo route add default gw 192.168.1.1

Delete a route:
sudo route del default gw 192.168.1.1

hostname

View the current hostname:
hostname

Change the hostname to myserver:
sudo hostname myserver

nmcli (for systems using NetworkManager)

View the status of network devices:
nmcli dev status

Activate a network connection:
nmcli con up <connection_name>

Deactivate a network connection:
nmcli con down <connection_name>

Show available Wi-Fi networks:

nmcli dev wifi list

netstat

View network connections:
netstat -tuln
This shows active listening ports and network connections.

View all active connections (including established ones):
netstat -an

ss (Socket Statictics)
ss is similar to netstat but provides more detailed information and is generally faster.

View active connections:
ss -tuln

Show all connections with process information:
ss -plnt

ping

Test connectivity to a remote host:
ping 8.8.8.8

This sends ICMP echo requests to Google's DNS server (8.8.8.8).

Ping a domain:
ping google.com

Ping continuously:
ping -t google.com

traceroute

Trace the route packets take to a destination:
traceroute google.com
This shows each hop between your machine and the destination.

dig (Domain Information Groper)

Query DNS for a domain name:
dig google.com

View the DNS records for a domain:
dig google.com any

nslookup

Query DNS for a domain name:
nslookup google.com

ifup and ifdown (Debian-based systems)

Bring an interface up:
sudo ifup eth0

Bring an interface down:
sudo ifdown eth0

systemctl

Check the status of the NetworkManager service:
systemctl status NetworkManager

Restart NetworkManager:
sudo systemctl restart NetworkManager

ip route

View routing information:
ip route show

Add a static route:
sudo ip route add 192.168.2.0/24 via 192.168.1.1
Delete a route:
sudo ip route del 192.168.2.0/24

ethtool
ethtool is used for querying and controlling network device parameters.

Show network interface settings:
sudo ethtool eth0

Change speed and duplex of an interface:
sudo ethtool -s eth0 speed 1000 duplex full

tcpdump
tcpdump is a packet analyzer, useful for capturing and analyzing network traffic.

Capture packets on an interface:
sudo tcpdump -i eth0

Capture specific traffic (e.g., HTTP):
sudo tcpdump -i eth0 port 80

iwconfig (for wireless interfaces)

View wireless network settings:
iwconfig

Change the wireless mode or SSID:
sudo iwconfig wlan0 essid "MyNetwork"

host

Find the IP address of a domain:
host google.com

curl

curl is useful for transferring data over various protocols, including HTTP, FTP, and more.

Fetch a web page:
curl **https://www.google.com**

route (for older systems)

View the routing table:
route -n

Add a route:

```
sudo route add -net 192.168.1.0 netmask 255.255.255.0 gw
192.168.0.1
```

Testing Connectivity

Testing connectivity is a crucial part of network troubleshooting in Linux, and several tools are available to assess the state of network connections. The ping command is one of the simplest and most commonly used tools, allowing you to send ICMP Echo Requests to a remote host to check if it's reachable. For example, ping google.com will test connectivity to Google's servers. The traceroute command goes a step further, showing the path that packets take to reach a destination, highlighting each router or hop along the way, which is useful for identifying where delays or failures occur. mtr combines the functionality of both ping and traceroute, providing a real-time, continuously updated view of the route packets take to a target and their latency at each hop, such as mtr google.com. Finally, netcat (often abbreviated as nc) is a versatile networking tool that can be used to test specific ports for connectivity.

For example, nc -zv google.com 80 tests whether port 80 (HTTP) is open and accessible on Google's server. Together, these tools provide a comprehensive suite for diagnosing connectivity issues at different levels of the network stack.

ping

Test connectivity to a remote host (e.g., Google's DNS server):
ping google.com
This sends ICMP Echo Requests to google.com and waits for responses.

Ping a specific IP address:
ping 8.8.8.8
This tests connectivity to Google's public DNS server by IP address.

Ping continuously (without stopping):
ping -t google.com
This sends continuous ping requests until manually stopped.

Ping with a specific number of requests (e.g., 4):
ping -c 4 google.com

traceroute

Trace the route to a destination (e.g., google.com):
traceroute google.com
This shows the path taken by packets from your computer to google.com, including each hop and the time it took to reach it.

Use a specific port for the trace:

traceroute -p 80 google.com
This traces the route to google.com, specifically over port 80 (HTTP).

mtr (combines ping and traceroute)

Run a basic MTR test:
mtr google.com
This will show a real-time, continuously updated view of the path and latency of each hop to google.com.

Run MTR with a specified number of pings per hop:
mtr -c 10 google.com
This sends 10 pings per hop, providing more detailed data on each hop's performance.

netcat (nc)

Test if a specific port is open (e.g., HTTP port 80 on google.com):
nc -zv google.com 80
This checks if port 80 (HTTP) is open on google.com. The -z flag tells nc to scan without sending any data, and -v enables verbose output to show whether the port is open or closed.

Test connectivity to a specific IP and port:
nc -zv 8.8.8.8 53

This checks if port 53 (DNS) is open on Google's DNS server at IP address 8.8.8.8.

Create a simple TCP connection to a remote host:
nc google.com 80
This opens a connection to port 80 (HTTP) on google.com. You can then type HTTP commands like GET / HTTP/1.1 to test the server response.

Managing Connections

Managing network connections on a Linux system is essential for monitoring and troubleshooting active services and network traffic. The ss (socket statistics) command is a powerful tool for displaying detailed information about network connections, offering more speed and functionality than the older netstat.

For instance, ss -tuln lists all active listening TCP and UDP ports along with their associated addresses and states. Similarly, netstat can be used to view active connections, listening ports, and routing tables; the command netstat -tuln displays TCP/UDP connections in a listening state. lsof -i is another valuable tool that lists all open network connections and the processes using them.

By running lsof -i, you can identify which processes are communicating over the network, making it useful for debugging issues related to unauthorized or unexpected connections. Together, these commands provide a comprehensive view of network activity, helping administrators manage and troubleshoot network connections effectively.

ss
List all listening TCP and UDP ports:
ss -tuln
This command shows all active TCP and UDP connections in the listening state, including the local address, port, and the state of the connection.

Display more detailed information about all TCP connections:
ss -t -a
This lists all TCP connections, including those that are established and listening.

Show listening sockets with process information:
ss -tulnp
This displays all listening ports along with the process IDs (PID) and process names associated with the connections.

netstat

Display active listening TCP and UDP ports:
netstat -tuln
This shows all listening TCP and UDP ports, with the local address and port number.

Show all active network connections, including established ones:
netstat -an
This lists all connections (including established ones) along with their IP addresses and ports.

Show network statistics (including connections):
netstat -s
This provides a summary of network statistics such as TCP connections, packet counts, and errors.

lsof -i

List all open network connections:
lsof -i
This command displays all open Internet connections and the processes that opened them.

List processes using a specific port (e.g., port 80):
lsof -i :80
This shows which processes are using port 80 (typically HTTP).

Show connections for a specific protocol (e.g., TCP):
lsof -i tcp
This lists all open TCP connections and the associated processes.

Find a specific process by its PID:
lsof -i -p <PID>

Replace <PID> with the process ID to show the open network connections of that specific process.

SSH and Remote Access

SSH (Secure Shell) and its associated tools, such as scp (Secure Copy) and rsync, are fundamental for secure remote access and file management on Linux systems. ssh is used to securely log into remote machines over a network, encrypting the entire session to ensure confidentiality and integrity. For example, ssh user@hostname connects to a remote server using the specified username. scp allows for secure file transfers between a local machine and a remote machine, or between two remote systems. For instance, scp file.txt user@hostname:/path/to/destination copies a local file to a remote destination. rsync is another powerful tool for efficient file synchronization and backup, especially useful for large directories.

Unlike scp, rsync only transfers the differences between files, reducing data transfer time. A typical command might be rsync -avz /local/dir/ user@hostname:/remote/dir/, which synchronizes directories while preserving permissions and compressing data for efficiency. Together, these tools provide essential capabilities for managing remote systems and securely transferring files across networks.

ssh (Secure Shell)

Log in to a remote server:
ssh user@hostname
This command logs into the remote machine with the username user at the specified hostname (either IP address or domain name).

Log in to a remote server with a custom port (e.g., port 2222):
ssh -p 2222 user@hostname
This connects to hostname using port 2222 instead of the default SSH port 22.

Execute a command on a remote server without fully logging in:
ssh user@hostname 'ls /var/www'
This runs the ls command on the remote server to list the contents of /var/www without starting a full interactive session.

scp (Secure Copy)

Copy a local file to a remote server:
scp file.txt user@hostname:/path/to/destination
This command copies file.txt from the local machine to the specified directory on the remote server.

Copy a file from a remote server to the local machine:
scp user@hostname:/path/to/file.txt /local/destination

This command copies file.txt from the remote server to the specified local directory.

Copy a directory recursively to a remote server:
scp -r /local/dir user@hostname:/path/to/destination
The -r flag copies the entire directory /local/dir (including its contents) to the remote server.

rsync (Remote Synchronization)

Sync a local directory with a remote directory (preserving permissions):
rsync -avz /local/dir/ user@hostname:/remote/dir/
The -a flag preserves permissions, symbolic links, and other file attributes, while -v enables verbose output, and -z compresses the data during transfer.

Sync a remote directory with a local directory (only transferring changed files):
rsync -avz user@hostname:/remote/dir/ /local/dir/
This command synchronizes the remote directory /remote/dir/ with the local directory /local/dir/, copying only the files that have changed since the last sync.

Exclude certain files or directories from the sync:
rsync -avz --exclude 'temp/' /local/dir/ user@hostname:/remote/dir/
This example excludes the temp/ directory from being transferred during the synchronization.

Run a dry-run to simulate the rsync operation:

rsync -avzn /local/dir/ user@hostname:/remote/dir/

The -n flag performs a dry run, showing what files would be transferred without actually making any changes.

Chapter 9: Managing Software and Packages

Managing software and packages on Linux systems is a critical task for system administrators and users, with different Linux distributions using distinct package management tools. These tools allow users to install, remove, and update software packages efficiently. For Debian-based distributions, such as Ubuntu, the primary package management tool is apt (Advanced Package Tool). With apt, users can easily install software by running commands like sudo apt install package-name. To keep the system up-to-date, sudo apt update fetches the latest package information, and sudo apt upgrade installs updates for all installed packages. apt also handles dependencies automatically, ensuring that all required libraries and packages are installed alongside the requested software.

Red Hat-based distributions, such as CentOS, Fedora, and RHEL, use a different set of tools for package management. The most common tool for these distributions is yum (Yellowdog Updater, Modified), though dnf (Dandified YUM) is the default package manager for newer versions of Fedora. These tools function similarly to apt, allowing users to install packages with sudo yum install package-name or sudo dnf install package-name in Fedora. Both tools manage package dependencies and ensure the proper installation of related software. Additionally, yum and dnf offer commands for updating software, such as sudo yum update or sudo dnf upgrade, keeping the system secure and current with the latest software releases.

For managing packages outside of the default system repositories or for those requiring specific versions, tools like snap and flatpak have become increasingly popular. These tools allow users to install containerized applications, which are isolated from the rest of the system, making them easy to update and manage across different Linux distributions. Unlike traditional package managers, snap and flatpak provide a consistent method of software installation, regardless of the underlying Linux distribution. Together, these package management tools provide a flexible and reliable framework for managing software on Linux systems, ensuring that all systems remain up-to-date, secure, and capable of running the latest applications.

Package Management Systems

Package management systems are essential tools for installing, updating, and removing software packages on Linux distributions. apt (Advanced Package Tool) is used by Debian-based distributions like Ubuntu and handles package installations, updates, and dependencies with commands like apt install and apt upgrade. yum and its successor dnf (Dandified YUM) are used on Red Hat-based systems such as CentOS, Fedora, and RHEL, offering similar functionality with commands like yum install or dnf install for package management. zypper is the package manager for openSUSE, allowing users to manage software with commands such as zypper install and zypper update. For Arch Linux and its derivatives, pacman is the preferred package manager, known for its simplicity and speed, offering commands like pacman -S to install packages and pacman -Syu for system updates. These package managers provide a reliable and streamlined way to manage software across different Linux distributions, ensuring users can easily maintain up-to-date systems with minimal effort.

apt (Debian-based systems like Ubuntu)

Install a package:
sudo apt install package-name
This command installs the specified package, replacing package-name with the name of the software you want to install.

Update package list:
sudo apt update
This fetches the latest package information from repositories, ensuring you have the most up-to-date package list.

Upgrade all packages:
sudo apt upgrade
This updates all installed packages to their latest available versions.

yum (Red Hat-based systems like CentOS)

Install a package:
sudo yum install package-name

This command installs the specified package on systems using yum.

Update package list and upgrade packages:
sudo yum update
This updates all installed packages to the latest version available from the repositories.

Remove a package:
sudo yum remove package-name
This removes the specified package from the system.

dnf (Fedora, CentOS/RHEL 8 and above)

Install a package:
sudo dnf install package-name
Similar to yum, but dnf is the more modern and improved version of the package manager.

Update all packages:
sudo dnf update
This command updates all installed packages to the latest available versions from repositories.

Search for a package:
dnf search package-name
This searches for the specified package in the available repositories.

zypper (openSUSE)

Install a package:
sudo zypper install package-name
This installs the specified package on openSUSE systems.

Update all packages:
sudo zypper update
This command updates all installed packages to their latest versions.

Remove a package:
sudo zypper remove package-name
This removes the specified package from the system.

pacman (Arch Linux)

Install a package:
sudo pacman -S package-name
This command installs the specified package on Arch Linux systems.

Update the system:
sudo pacman -Syu
This updates the system by synchronizing the package database and upgrading all installed packages.

Search for a package:
pacman -Ss package-name
This searches for the package in the Arch repositories.

Installing, Updating, and Removing Packages

Installing, updating, and removing packages are fundamental tasks in managing a Linux system, and each distribution provides specific commands to perform these actions. For Debian-based distributions like Ubuntu, apt-get install package-name is used to install new software, while apt-get update refreshes the package index to fetch the latest available versions. To update all installed packages, apt-get upgrade is used. In Red Hat-based systems such as CentOS, yum install package-name installs a package, and yum update upgrades all installed software to the latest versions. Fedora and newer Red Hat-based systems use dnf (Dandified YUM), where dnf update updates packages, and dnf install package-name installs new software. On openSUSE, zypper is the package manager, with zypper install package-name for installations and zypper remove package-name to uninstall a package. These package management commands are essential for keeping systems up-to-date, secure, and running the necessary software.

Debian-based distributions (Ubuntu, etc.) — Using apt-get

Install a package:
sudo apt-get install package-name
Example: To install curl, run:
sudo apt-get install curl

Update package list:
sudo apt-get update

This command updates the package index to ensure you get the latest package versions available.

Upgrade all packages:
sudo apt-get upgrade
This updates all the installed packages to their latest versions available from the repositories.

Remove a package:
sudo apt-get remove package-name
Example: To remove curl, run:
sudo apt-get remove curl

Red Hat-based distributions (CentOS, RHEL, Fedora) — using yum

Install a package:
sudo yum install package-name
Example: To install httpd, run:
sudo yum install httpd

Update all packages:
sudo yum update
This command updates all installed packages to the latest versions.

Remove a package:
sudo yum remove package-name
Example: To remove httpd, run:
sudo yum remove httpd

Fedora (newer Red Hat-based systems) — using dnf

Install a package:
sudo dnf install package-name
Example: To install nginx, run:
sudo dnf install nginx

Update all packages:
sudo dnf update
This will update all installed packages on your Fedora system to the latest versions.

Remove a package:
sudo dnf remove package-name
Example: To remove nginx, run:
sudo dnf remove nginx

openSUSE — using zypper

Install a package:
sudo zypper install package-name
Example: To install vlc, run:
sudo zypper install vlc

Update all packages:
sudo zypper update
This command updates all the installed packages to the latest available versions.

Remove a package:
sudo zypper remove package-name
Example: To remove vlc, run:
sudo zypper remove vlc

Managing Repositories

Managing repositories is an essential part of maintaining a Linux system, as it determines where software packages are sourced from. On Debian-based systems like Ubuntu, add-apt-repository is used to add new repositories to the system, allowing users to install software from additional sources beyond the default ones. For example, sudo add-apt-repository ppa:repository-name/ppa adds a PPA (Personal Package Archive) to the system. To authenticate and manage repository keys, apt-key is used to add, list, or remove keys, ensuring secure package installations. On Red Hat-based systems like CentOS, yum-config-manager is used to manage repository configurations. With commands like yum-config-manager --add-repo repository-url, users can add external repositories, and yum-config-manager --disable repo-name can disable specific repositories. These tools help ensure that a system can access the required software from trusted and secure repositories while offering flexibility in sourcing packages.

Debian-based systems (Ubuntu, etc.) — using add-apt-repository and apt-key

Add a repository (PPA) using add-apt-repository:
sudo add-apt-repository ppa:repository-name/ppa

Example: To add a PPA for a specific version of Python:
sudo add-apt-repository ppa:deadsnakes/ppa

Add a repository key using apt-key:
sudo apt-key adv --keyserver keyserver.ubuntu.com --recv-keys KEY_ID

Example: To add a GPG key for a repository:
sudo apt-key adv --keyserver keyserver.ubuntu.com --recv-keys 3B4FE6ACC0B21F32

List all repository keys:
sudo apt-key list
This command lists all the GPG keys used to authenticate packages from repositories.

Remove a repository key:
sudo apt-key del KEY_ID

Example: To remove the key:
sudo apt-key del 3B4FE6ACC0B21F32

Red Hat-based systems (CentOS, RHEL, Fedora) — using yum-config-manager

Add a repository using yum-config-manager:
sudo yum-config-manager --add-repo repository-url
Example: To add the EPEL (Extra Packages for Enterprise Linux) repository:
sudo yum-config-manager --add-repo
https://dl.fedoraproject.org/pub/epel/7/x86_64/epel-release-7-11.noarch.rpm

Enable a repository:
sudo yum-config-manager --enable repository-name
Example: To enable the EPEL repository:
sudo yum-config-manager --enable epel

Disable a repository:
sudo yum-config-manager --disable repository-name
Example: To disable the EPEL repository:
sudo yum-config-manager --disable epel

List all repositories:
sudo yum repolist
This command shows a list of all enabled repositories on the system.

Chapter 10: Disk and Filesystem Management

Disk and filesystem management are critical tasks for maintaining the integrity, performance, and organization of storage on a Linux system. Linux provides a variety of tools and commands for managing disks and filesystems, allowing administrators to partition, format, and monitor disk usage efficiently. To manage disks, tools like fdisk or parted are used to create, delete, and modify disk partitions. For example, fdisk /dev/sda opens the partition table of the first disk (/dev/sda), allowing users to manipulate partitions. Once partitions are created, they need to be formatted with a filesystem using commands like mkfs (e.g., mkfs.ext4 /dev/sda1 to format a partition as ext4).

Once partitions are formatted, they can be mounted to specific directories on the filesystem using the mount command (e.g., mount /dev/sda1 /mnt). Linux also provides tools like lsblk, df, and du to monitor disk usage. lsblk lists all available block devices, while df shows filesystem disk space usage, and du helps determine the disk usage of specific directories or files. Filesystems can be managed and repaired using commands like fsck (e.g., fsck /dev/sda1 to check and repair a filesystem). Additionally, the partprobe command is used to inform the OS of partition table changes without needing a reboot.

For more advanced management, Logical Volume Manager (LVM) allows the creation of flexible, dynamic storage volumes, enabling users to resize partitions or group them together across physical disks. Tools like vgcreate, lvcreate, and lvextend are part of LVM's suite, providing granular control over storage allocation. These disk and filesystem management tools ensure that Linux systems remain efficient, organized, and capable of scaling to meet changing storage requirements.

Creating and Managing Partitions

Creating and managing partitions is a crucial aspect of disk management in Linux, and tools like fdisk, parted, and lsblk are essential for these tasks. fdisk is used to create, delete, and modify partitions on MBR (Master Boot Record) disks. For example, fdisk /dev/sda opens the partition table of the first disk and allows users to create new partitions or modify existing ones. parted, on the other hand, is a more advanced tool that supports both MBR and GPT (GUID Partition Table) disks, and offers additional features like resizing partitions. An example command is parted /dev/sda mkpart primary ext4 0% 50%, which creates a primary partition that spans the first 50% of the disk space. To list all available disks and partitions, lsblk is often used, providing a clear overview of block devices and their associated mount points. These tools allow users to effectively organize and allocate disk space according to system needs, ensuring proper partitioning for data storage and system use.

fdisk (For MBR Partitioning)

View the partition table:
sudo fdisk -l
This lists all the partitions on all connected disks.

Create a new partition:
sudo fdisk /dev/sda

After entering fdisk, you can type:
n to create a new partition
Select p for primary partition or e for extended partition
Choose the partition number, first sector, and last sector to define the size.
Type w to write the changes.

Delete a partition:
sudo fdisk /dev/sda
Then, type:
d to delete a partition
Choose the partition number to delete
Type w to save the changes.

parted (For MBR and GPT Partitioning)
View partition details:
sudo parted /dev/sda print
This shows the partition layout of /dev/sda.

Create a new partition:
sudo parted /dev/sda mkpart primary ext4 0% 50%

This creates a primary partition starting from 0% to 50% of the disk, with the ext4 filesystem.

Resize a partition:
sudo parted /dev/sda resizepart 1 100%
This resizes partition 1 to take up the full available space of the disk.

Delete a partition:
sudo parted /dev/sda rm 1
This deletes partition 1 on /dev/sda.

lsblk (List Block Devices)

List all block devices:
lsblk
This lists all block devices (disks and partitions) along with their sizes, mount points, and other details.

List block devices with more detailed information:
lsblk -f
This shows additional details, including filesystem types (e.g., ext4, xfs) and mount points.

List block devices with a specific disk:
lsblk /dev/sda
This shows only the partitions and details related to /dev/sda.

Mounting and Unmounting Filesystems

Mounting and unmounting filesystems are essential tasks for accessing and managing storage devices in Linux. The mount command is used to attach a filesystem to a specific directory (mount point) so that it can be accessed. For example, sudo mount /dev/sda1 /mnt mounts the partition /dev/sda1 to the /mnt directory. Once a filesystem is no longer needed, it can be safely detached using the umount command, such as sudo umount /mnt, which unmounts the filesystem from the specified directory. The df command is commonly used to display information about disk space usage for mounted filesystems. Running df -h shows the available and used space on all mounted filesystems in a human-readable format. Proper mounting and unmounting ensure data integrity and prevent filesystem corruption, especially when removing external storage devices or modifying partitions.

mount (Mount a Filesystem)

Mount a partition:
sudo mount /dev/sda1 /mnt
This command mounts the partition /dev/sda1 to the /mnt directory. After running this, the contents of /dev/sda1 will be accessible under /mnt.

Mount with a specific filesystem type:
sudo mount -t ext4 /dev/sda1 /mnt

Here, -t ext4 specifies that the filesystem type is ext4. This is useful if the system doesn't automatically detect the filesystem type.

Mount with read-only access:
sudo mount -o ro /dev/sda1 /mnt
The -o ro option mounts the filesystem in read-only mode, preventing any changes to the mounted data.

umount (Unmount a Filesystem)

Unmount a partition:
sudo umount /mnt
This unmounts the filesystem that was mounted at /mnt. The filesystem is safely detached from the directory, and it is no longer accessible until mounted again.

Unmount by device:
sudo umount /dev/sda1
Alternatively, you can unmount by specifying the device name directly.

Force unmount (use with caution):
sudo umount -f /mnt
The -f flag forces the unmount, useful if the device is busy or there's a problem with the filesystem. This option should be used carefully as it can cause data loss.

df (Disk Space Usage)

Display disk space usage:
df
This shows disk space usage for all mounted filesystems in terms of total, used, and available space.

Display disk space in human-readable format:
df -h
The -h option shows the space usage in a human-readable format, such as KB, MB, or GB, making it easier to understand the size of filesystems.

Display disk space for a specific filesystem:
df -h /mnt
This shows the disk space usage for the filesystem mounted at /mnt.

Checking Disk Health and Filesystem Integrity

Checking disk health and filesystem integrity is essential for maintaining the reliability of storage devices in Linux. The fsck (File System Consistency Check) command is used to scan and repair filesystems for errors. For example, running sudo fsck /dev/sda1 checks and repairs the filesystem on the partition /dev/sda1 if any inconsistencies or corruption are found. The smartctl command is part of the smartmontools package and allows users to monitor the health of hard drives and solid-state drives (SSDs) using S.M.A.R.T. (Self-Monitoring, Analysis, and Reporting Technology). An example command, sudo smartctl -a /dev/sda, retrieves detailed health information, including temperature, error rates, and potential issues with the drive. For checking bad sectors on a disk, badblocks can be used to scan for physical defects. For example, sudo badblocks -v /dev/sda runs a non-destructive scan of the disk to identify any bad blocks, which could lead to data loss or performance degradation. Together, these tools provide comprehensive means to ensure that both the filesystem and physical disk are in good health, minimizing the risk of data loss and ensuring system stability.

fsck (File System Consistency Check)

Check and repair a filesystem:
sudo fsck /dev/sda1
This checks and repairs the filesystem on /dev/sda1. If errors are found, it will prompt you to fix them.

Automatically fix filesystem errors:
sudo fsck -y /dev/sda1
The -y flag automatically answers "yes" to all prompts, allowing fsck to fix errors without user intervention.

Check a filesystem without modifying it:
sudo fsck -n /dev/sda1
The -n flag runs fsck in a read-only mode (no changes are made), simply reporting any errors without fixing them.

smartctl (S.M.A.R.T. Monitoring)

View detailed S.M.A.R.T. status:
sudo smartctl -a /dev/sda
This command retrieves detailed health information about the /dev/sda drive, such as error rates, temperature, and any other potential issues.

Run a short self-test:
sudo smartctl -t short /dev/sda
This initiates a quick self-test on the drive, which typically takes a few minutes and checks for basic health issues.

Run a long self-test:
sudo smartctl -t long /dev/sda
The -t long option runs a more thorough, extended test, which can take several hours depending on the size and condition of the drive.

badblocks (Scan for Bad Sectors)

Scan a disk for bad sectors (non-destructive):
sudo badblocks -v /dev/sda
This command performs a read-only scan of /dev/sda to find bad blocks (sectors) on the disk. The -v option provides a verbose output showing progress and any detected bad blocks.

Scan and mark bad blocks on the disk:
sudo badblocks -w -v /dev/sda

The -w option runs a write test, which writes patterns to the disk and checks for bad sectors. Be cautious, as this will overwrite data on the disk. This test is more thorough than the read-only scan.

Save bad blocks to a file:
sudo badblocks -v /dev/sda > badblocks.txt
This command saves any detected bad blocks to a file (badblocks.txt), which can later be used for further diagnostics or used with fsck to mark the bad blocks in the filesystem.

Chapter 11: Backup and Compression

Backup and compression are vital components of data management, ensuring that valuable information is preserved and stored efficiently. Backup refers to creating copies of important files or entire systems to protect against data loss, whether due to hardware failure, human error, or disasters. In Linux, tools like rsync and tar are commonly used for backing up data. The rsync command allows for incremental backups, meaning it only copies the files that have changed, making it efficient for regular backups. For example, rsync -av /source /destination copies files from /source to /destination while preserving file permissions and structure. The tar command is another powerful tool for creating compressed archive backups. A typical use is tar -czvf backup.tar.gz /important_folder, which creates a compressed .tar.gz archive of the /important_folder. This archive can then be stored in a secure location.

Compression plays a critical role in reducing the size of backup files, making storage more efficient and quicker for transmission over networks. Linux provides several compression utilities like gzip, bzip2, and xz, which can be used in conjunction with backup tools. For example, gzip is commonly used to compress files and archives, as seen in the tar example above. bzip2 and xz often provide higher compression ratios at the cost of more processing power, which can be useful for archiving large datasets. To compress an existing file using gzip, one can use the command gzip file.txt, which results in a smaller file.txt.gz file. When creating backups, combining backup tools with compression ensures that data is both secure and stored in a space-efficient manner, facilitating easier recovery and transport.

Creating Backups

Creating backups is an essential practice in data management, and in Linux, several tools like tar, rsync, and dd are commonly used for this purpose. The tar command is frequently used for creating compressed archive backups of files and directories, providing a convenient way to store data in a single file. For example, tar -czvf backup.tar.gz /home/user/data creates a compressed .tar.gz archive of the /home/user/data directory, which can be easily stored or transferred. The rsync command is particularly useful for incremental backups, where only the changed or new files are copied, making it ideal for regular backups.

An example command would be rsync -av /source /backup, which synchronizes files from /source to /backup, preserving file attributes and permissions. The dd command is a low-level tool used for creating byte-for-byte backups of entire drives or partitions, often employed for system cloning or disk imaging. For instance, sudo dd if=/dev/sda of=/dev/sdb bs=64K conv=noerror,sync creates a backup of /dev/sda (the source drive) to /dev/sdb (the destination drive), using a block size of 64KB. These tools provide flexibility in creating backups, whether it's for individual files, directories, or entire disks, ensuring that data can be restored in case of loss or failure.

tar (Tape Archive)

Create a compressed backup of a directory:
tar -czvf backup.tar.gz /home/user/data
This command creates a compressed .tar.gz archive of the /home/user/data directory and saves it as backup.tar.gz. The -c option creates the archive, -z compresses it with gzip, -v shows verbose output, and -f specifies the output file.

Create a backup of multiple directories:
tar -czvf backup.tar.gz /home/user/data /home/user/docs
This command backs up both /home/user/data and /home/user/docs into a single compressed archive.

Extract files from a .tar.gz backup:
tar -xzvf backup.tar.gz
This extracts the contents of backup.tar.gz to the current directory, using the -x option to extract the files.

rsync (Remote Synchronization)

Create a backup of a directory to another location:
rsync -av /home/user/data /backup/location
This command synchronizes the /home/user/data directory to /backup/location, preserving file attributes (-a for archive mode) and providing verbose output (-v).

Create an incremental backup:
rsync -av --delete /home/user/data /backup/location

The --delete flag removes files from the backup location that no longer exist in the source directory, effectively creating an incremental backup where only changes are copied.

Backup over a network to a remote server:
rsync -av /home/user/data user@remote_server:/backup/location
This command backs up /home/user/data to a remote server at remote_server, saving it to /backup/location on the remote machine.

dd (Data Description)

Create a byte-for-byte backup of a drive:
sudo dd if=/dev/sda of=/dev/sdb bs=64K conv=noerror,sync
This command creates an exact copy of the source drive (/dev/sda) to the destination drive (/dev/sdb), using a block size of 64KB. The conv=noerror,sync option tells dd to continue reading even if errors are encountered and to synchronize input and output blocks.

Create a backup of a partition to an image file:
sudo dd if=/dev/sda1 of=/path/to/backup.img bs=4M
This command backs up the /dev/sda1 partition to a file named backup.img with a block size of 4MB.

Restore a backup image to a partition:
sudo dd if=/path/to/backup.img of=/dev/sda1 bs=4M
This command restores the backup.img file to the /dev/sda1 partition, using the same block size as when the backup was created.

Compressing and Archiving

Compressing and archiving are crucial for managing and storing data efficiently, and Linux provides several tools for these tasks, including gzip, bzip2, xz, zip, unzip, and tar. gzip is a widely used compression tool that reduces the size of files using the .gz format, while bzip2 offers higher compression ratios, producing .bz2 files, but at the cost of slower compression speeds. xz provides even better compression, creating .xz files, often used for large datasets due to its superior compression capabilities. zip is commonly used for creating compressed archives that can be easily opened on various platforms, producing .zip files, and unzip is used to extract files from these archives. On the other hand, tar is not a compression tool by itself but is often used in combination with compression tools like gzip, bzip2, or xz to archive multiple files into a single compressed file. For example, tar -czvf archive.tar.gz /folder creates a .tar.gz archive of the /folder directory, while tar -xjvf archive.tar.bz2 extracts a .tar.bz2 file. These tools are essential for backing up, transferring, and organizing files in a space-efficient manner.

gzip (GNU zip)

Compress a file:
gzip file.txt
This command compresses file.txt into a file.txt.gz file. The original file.txt is removed by default.

Decompress a .gz file:

gunzip file.txt.gz

This command decompresses the file.txt.gz file back to its original file.txt.

bzip2

Compress a file:

bzip2 file.txt

This command compresses file.txt into file.txt.bz2.

Decompress a .bz2 file:

bunzip2 file.txt.bz2

This decompresses file.txt.bz2 back to the original file.txt.

xz

Compress a file:

xz file.txt

This command compresses file.txt into file.txt.xz.

Decompress a .xz file:

unxz file.txt.xz

This decompresses file.txt.xz back to the original file.txt.

zip

Create a .zip archive of a file or directory:
zip archive.zip file1.txt file2.txt
This command creates a archive.zip containing file1.txt and file2.txt.

Create a .zip archive of an entire directory:
zip -r archive.zip /folder
This creates a archive.zip file that contains all the files and subdirectories inside /folder.

Extract a .zip archive:
unzip archive.zip
This extracts the contents of archive.zip into the current directory.

tar (Tape Archive)

Create a .tar.gz archive (gzip compression):
tar -czvf archive.tar.gz /folder
This command creates a compressed archive archive.tar.gz of the /folder directory.

Create a .tar.bz2 archive (bzip2 compression):
tar -cjvf archive.tar.bz2 /folder
This creates a compressed .tar.bz2 archive of /folder.

Create a .tar.xz archive (xz compression):
tar -cJvf archive.tar.xz /folder

This creates a compressed .tar.xz archive of /folder.

Extract a .tar.gz archive:
tar -xzvf archive.tar.gz
This extracts the contents of archive.tar.gz.

Extract a .tar.bz2 archive:
tar -xjvf archive.tar.bz2
This extracts the contents of archive.tar.bz2.

Extract a .tar.xz archive:
tar -xJvf archive.tar.xz
This extracts the contents of archive.tar.xz.

Summary of archive utilities

gzip: Best for compressing individual files into .gz.

bzip2: Provides higher compression ratios than gzip, producing .bz2 files.

xz: Offers even better compression than bzip2, creating .xz files.

zip: Widely used for creating .zip archives, including directories, and can be extracted on many platforms.

tar: Primarily used to create archives (tarballs), often combined with compression tools like gzip, bzip2, and xz for efficient storage.

Restoring from Backups

Restoring from backups is essential for recovering lost or corrupted data, and Linux provides powerful tools like tar and rsync for this purpose. When extracting archives, tar is commonly used to restore compressed backup files, such as .tar.gz or .tar.bz2 files. For example, the command tar -xzvf backup.tar.gz extracts the contents of a .tar.gz archive, restoring the original files and directories. On the other hand, rsync is a versatile tool for efficiently copying and synchronizing directories and files between locations, making it ideal for incremental backups. To restore a directory from a remote backup using rsync, you could run a command like rsync -avz user@remote:/path/to/backup/ /local/restore/, which copies the files from the remote backup directory to a local directory, ensuring the structure and permissions are preserved. These tools are invaluable for ensuring data integrity and rapid recovery when needed.

tar (Tape Archive)

Extracting a .tar.gz archive (gzip-compressed) to restore files:
tar -xzvf backup.tar.gz
This command extracts the contents of backup.tar.gz into the current directory. The options -xzvf mean:
x: Extract the archive
z: Decompress with gzip
v: Verbose output (shows files being extracted)
f: Specifies the archive file (backup.tar.gz)

Extracting a .tar.bz2 archive (bzip2-compressed):
tar -xjvf backup.tar.bz2
This extracts a .tar.bz2 archive using bzip2 compression.

Extracting a .tar.xz archive (xz-compressed):
tar -xJvf backup.tar.xz
This extracts a .tar.xz archive using xz compression.

Extracting to a specific directory:
tar -xzvf backup.tar.gz -C /path/to/restore/
This restores the contents of backup.tar.gz into the /path/to/restore/ directory instead of the current directory.

rsync (Remote Synchronization)

Restoring files from a remote server to a local directory:
rsync -avz user@remote:/path/to/backup/ /local/restore/
This command synchronizes the files from the remote server at /path/to/backup/ to the local directory /local/restore/.

The options -avz mean:
a: Archive mode (preserves permissions, symbolic links, etc.)
v: Verbose output (shows details of the files being transferred)
z: Compresses file data during the transfer

Restoring specific files from a remote server:
rsync -avz user@remote:/path/to/backup/file1.txt /local/restore/

This command restores only file1.txt from the remote backup to the local directory.

Restoring from a local directory to another local directory:
rsync -avz /path/to/backup/ /local/restore/
This synchronizes the backup directory /path/to/backup/ to /local/restore/ on the local machine.

Using rsync for incremental backups:
rsync -avz --delete /path/to/source/ /path/to/backup/
This command updates the backup with any changes in the source directory and deletes files from the backup that no longer exist in the source directory (for an exact mirror of the source).

Chapter 12: Hardware Detection and Management

Hardware detection and management in Linux involves identifying and managing the hardware components of a system, such as the CPU, memory, storage devices, and peripherals. Linux provides a variety of tools to detect hardware and gather detailed information about system components. For example, the lshw (list hardware) command provides a comprehensive overview of the hardware configuration, including the CPU, RAM, disk drives, network interfaces, and more. Running sudo lshw -short gives a summarized list of hardware devices. For detecting specific hardware, tools like lscpu display information about the CPU architecture, while lsblk lists block devices, showing information about storage devices and partitions. The lspci command identifies PCI devices, such as graphics cards and network adapters, while lsusb provides details about USB devices connected to the system.

For managing and interacting with devices, udevadm is useful for controlling device events, and hdparm helps manage hard drive parameters. Additionally, the dmidecode command reveals details from the system's DMI (Desktop Management Interface) table, which can include information about the motherboard, BIOS, and other hardware specifics. These tools are crucial for system administrators and users to manage hardware configurations, troubleshoot issues, and optimize system performance.

Checking Installed Hardware

Checking installed hardware in Linux is essential for understanding the system's components and ensuring everything is functioning properly. Several commands can be used to gather detailed information about the installed hardware. The lshw command provides a comprehensive list of hardware, including details about the CPU, memory, storage, and network interfaces. For more specific information, lscpu displays CPU architecture details, while lsblk lists all block devices, showing storage devices and partitions. The lspci command identifies PCI devices, such as graphics cards and network cards, and lsusb shows information about USB devices connected to the system. Additionally, dmidecode extracts data from the system's BIOS, providing valuable information about the motherboard, BIOS version, and other hardware specifics. These commands are useful for system administrators and users to ensure that all hardware is correctly detected and configured.

lshw (List Hardware)

List all installed hardware in a detailed format:
sudo lshw
This command will display detailed information about the system's hardware, including CPU, memory, storage devices, and network interfaces. You can use sudo to get detailed access to all hardware components.

List hardware in a short format:
sudo lshw -short
This command shows a brief summary of hardware components.

lscpu (CPU Information)

Display detailed CPU information:
lscpu
This command will show information about the CPU architecture, including the number of cores, threads, CPU model, architecture type, and more.

lsblk (List Block Devices)

List all block devices, including storage and partitions:
lsblk
This will show all storage devices, their partitions, and mount points. It provides a clear view of the disk layout.

Show more detailed information (including filesystem types):
lsblk -f
This command adds the filesystem information to the output, making it easier to identify filesystem types for each partition.

lspci (List PCI Devices)

List all PCI devices (e.g., network adapters, graphics cards):
lspci
This command lists all the PCI devices on your system, such as graphics cards, network adapters, and sound cards.

Show detailed information about a specific PCI device:
lspci -v
The -v (verbose) option provides more detailed information about each device.

lsusb (List USB Devices)

List all USB devices connected to the system:
lsusb
This command lists all USB devices, such as printers, USB drives, and keyboards, connected to the system.

dmidecode (DMI Table Decoder)

Show information about the system's hardware (e.g., motherboard, BIOS):
sudo dmidecode
This command extracts information from the system's DMI table, revealing details about the motherboard, BIOS version, system manufacturer, and other important hardware information.

Show specific information (e.g., BIOS version):

sudo dmidecode -t bios

This command filters the output to show only BIOS-related information, such as version and release date.

CPU Info

To check CPU information in Linux, the lscpu and cat /proc/cpuinfo commands are commonly used. The lscpu command provides a concise overview of the CPU architecture, including the number of cores, threads, CPU model, clock speed, and cache size. It presents the data in an easily readable format, making it ideal for a quick check of CPU details. On the other hand, cat /proc/cpuinfo displays detailed information about each CPU core, including the processor model, vendor ID, core frequency, cache size, and flags. While lscpu provides a high-level summary, cat /proc/cpuinfo offers a more granular view, listing specific attributes for each CPU core in the system. Both tools are essential for system administrators and users seeking to understand their system's processing power and configuration.

lscpu (CPU Information Overview)

Display CPU details in a concise format:
lscpu
This will provide a summary of CPU details, including the architecture, number of CPUs, cores, threads, CPU model, clock speed, and cache size. For example:
Architecture: x86_64

```
CPU(s):          4
On-line CPU(s) list:  0-3
Model name:       Intel(R) Core(TM) i7-9700K CPU @ 3.60GHz
CPU MHz:         3600.000
Hypervisor vendor:   KVM
```

cat /proc/cpuinfo (Detailed CPU Information)

Display detailed information about the CPU(s):

cat /proc/cpuinfo

This command provides extensive information about each CPU core on your system, such as the processor model, cores, cache size, and flags. Here's an example of what the output might look like:

```
processor      : 0
vendor_id      : GenuineIntel
cpu family     : 6
model          : 158
model name     : Intel(R) Core(TM) i7-9700K CPU @ 3.60GHz
stepping       : 10
microcode      : 0xea
cpu MHz        : 3600.000
cache size     : 12288 KB
physical id    : 0
siblings       : 8
core id        : 0
cpu cores      : 4
apicid         : 0
```

Display specific CPU information for a particular core (e.g., CPU 1):

cat /proc/cpuinfo | grep -A 10 "processor 1"

This will display details for the second CPU core (processor 1) and show attributes like its frequency, model, and cache. Both lscpu and cat /proc/cpuinfo are valuable for inspecting the CPU configuration in Linux, with lscpu offering a more summarized view and cat /proc/cpuinfo providing detailed information for each processor in the system.

Memory Info

To check memory information in Linux, the free and cat /proc/meminfo commands are widely used. The free command provides a quick summary of the system's memory usage, displaying the total, used, free, shared, buffer/cache, and available memory in both kilobytes (KB) and megabytes (MB). It also shows swap space usage, which is useful for monitoring system performance.

For more detailed memory statistics, cat /proc/meminfo displays a comprehensive list of memory-related data, including the total physical memory, free memory, buffers, cached memory, and memory allocated to specific kernel processes. This command provides deeper insights into memory consumption, helping system administrators diagnose potential memory-related issues. Both commands are essential tools for monitoring system resources and ensuring optimal memory usage.

free (Memory Usage Summary)

Display memory usage in a human-readable format:
free -h
This will display the memory usage with human-readable units (e.g., MB or GB). Example output:

	total	used	free	shared	buff/cache	available
Mem:	16G	4.3G	7.1G	249M	4.6G	11G
Swap:	4G	0B	4G			

This shows the total memory, memory in use, free memory, swap usage, and available memory.

Display memory usage in kilobytes:
free -k
This will show the memory values in kilobytes (KB).

cat /proc/meminfo (Detailed Memory Information)

Display detailed memory information:
cat /proc/meminfo
This will provide a comprehensive view of the system's memory usage. Example output:
makefile
Copy code

```
MemTotal:      16324328 kB
MemFree:        7421044 kB
MemAvailable:  11305664 kB
Buffers:        282004 kB
Cached:        4121896 kB
SwapCached:         0 kB
Active:        6205440 kB
Inactive:      2449964 kB
```

Filter output to show specific memory data (e.g., total memory):
cat /proc/meminfo | grep MemTotal
This will display only the total amount of memory:

MemTotal: 16324328 kB

Both free and cat /proc/meminfo are valuable commands for inspecting memory usage in Linux. free gives a quick summary, while cat /proc/meminfo provides detailed information about different aspects of memory usage.

Disk Drives

To manage and inspect disk drives in Linux, the lsblk, fdisk -l, and blkid commands are essential tools. The lsblk command lists all block devices (such as hard drives, SSDs, and USB drives) in a tree-like format, showing their device names, sizes, and mount points, making it easy to view the overall disk structure. For more detailed partition information, fdisk -l displays a list of all the partitions on your system along with their sizes, types, and other attributes. It's a useful tool for checking partition layouts and verifying disk configurations. Meanwhile, blkid provides detailed information about each block device, such as UUIDs (Universally Unique Identifiers), file system types, and labels, which is particularly useful for mounting devices or editing configurations in /etc/fstab. Together, these commands offer a comprehensive view of disk drives, their partitions, and their configurations on a

Linux system.

lsblk (List Block Devices)

List all block devices with mount points:
lsblk

This will display a tree-like structure of block devices, including hard drives, partitions, and mount points. Example output:

```
NAME   MAJ:MIN RM  SIZE RO TYPE MOUNTPOINT
sda    8:0   0 100G 0 disk
├─sda1 8:1   0  99G 0 part /mnt/data
└─sda2 8:2   0   1G 0 part [SWAP]
sdb    8:16  0 500G 0 disk /mnt/backup
```

List block devices with additional information like file system type:
lsblk -f

This will show file system types and UUIDs for each device:

```
NAME   FSTYPE LABEL UUID                          MOUNTPOINT
sda
├─sda1 ext4       1234abcd-56ef-7890-abcd-1234567890ab /mnt/data
└─sda2 swap       9876abcd-12ef-3456-abcd-1234567890ab [SWAP]
sdb   ext4       8765dcba-12ef-3456-abcd-1234567890ab /mnt/backup
```

fdisk -l (List Partitions)

Display detailed partition information for all disks:
sudo fdisk -l

This command shows the partitions of all connected disks.

Example output:

Disk /dev/sda: 100 GB
Sector size (logical/physical): 512 bytes / 512 bytes
Disk label type: gpt
Disk identifier: ABCD-1234

Device	Start	End	Sectors	Size	Type
/dev/sda1	2048	209919	207872	101M	EFI System
/dev/sda2	209920	1023999	1022080	500M	Linux filesystem

blkid (Show Block Device Information)

Display detailed information about block devices:

sudo blkid

This command shows the UUIDs, file system types, and labels of devices.

Example output:

/dev/sda1:   UUID="1234abcd-56ef-7890-abcd-1234567890ab"
TYPE="ext4" PARTLABEL="Primary" PARTUUID="abcd1234-5678-90ef-1234-567890abcdef"
/dev/sda2:   UUID="9876abcd-12ef-3456-abcd-1234567890ab"
TYPE="swap" PARTLABEL="Swap" PARTUUID="dcba4321-8765-90fe-4321-87654321abcdef"
/dev/sdb: UUID="8765dcba-12ef-3456-abcd-1234567890ab"
TYPE="ext4" PARTLABEL="Backup" PARTUUID="bacd4321-1234-5678-9abc-1234567890ab"

These commands help you inspect disk drives, check their partition layouts, file system types, and UUIDs, and manage them efficiently. lsblk is great for a high-level overview, fdisk -l provides detailed partitioning information, and blkid offers specifics about the file systems and their unique identifiers.

PCI Devices

The lspci command in Linux is used to display detailed information about the PCI (Peripheral Component Interconnect) devices on a system. This command lists all PCI devices, including network cards, graphics cards, storage controllers, sound cards, and more. It shows the device's vendor, model, and associated driver, helping users identify and troubleshoot hardware components. By default, lspci provides a concise output, but additional options can be used for more detailed information. For example, using lspci -v gives verbose output, including device configuration and memory details. The lspci -nn option adds the PCI vendor and device IDs to the output, which can be helpful for identifying hardware when dealing with compatibility issues. This tool is crucial for managing hardware and resolving driver-related issues on Linux systems.

Basic lspci Command

List all PCI devices:
lspci

This will display a list of PCI devices on your system, such as network cards, graphics cards, and sound cards:

00:00.0 Host bridge: Intel Corporation 6 Series Chipset Family DRAM Controller (rev 09)

00:02.0 VGA compatible controller: Intel Corporation 3rd Gen Core processor Graphics Controller (rev 09)

00:1f.2 SATA controller: Intel Corporation 7 Series Chipset Family SATA Controller (rev 04)

02:00.0 Network controller: Intel Corporation Wireless 7260 (rev 73)

Verbose Output (-v)

Show detailed information about each PCI device:
lspci -v

This gives a more detailed description of the devices, including memory regions, IRQs, and other hardware settings:

00:02.0 VGA compatible controller: Intel Corporation 3rd Gen Core processor Graphics Controller (rev 09)

DeviceName: Onboard IGD

Subsystem: Dell Device 055e

Flags: bus master, fast devsel, latency 0, IRQ 42

Memory at f0000000 (64-bit, non-prefetchable) [size=16M]

I/O ports at f000 [size=64]

Memory at f7d00000 (64-bit, prefetchable) [size=4M]

Adding Vendor and Device IDs (-nn)

Display PCI device information with vendor and device IDs:

lspci -nn

This will show the device and vendor IDs, which can be helpful for identifying devices, especially when troubleshooting:

00:00.0 Host bridge [0600]: Intel Corporation 6 Series Chipset Family DRAM Controller [8086:1c00] (rev 09)

00:02.0 VGA compatible controller [0300]: Intel Corporation 3rd Gen Core processor Graphics Controller [8086:0166] (rev 09)

00:1f.2 SATA controller [0106]: Intel Corporation 7 Series Chipset Family SATA Controller [8086:2822] (rev 04)

Display Specific Device Information (-s)

Show information for a specific PCI device by its address:
lspci -s 00:02.0

This command will show detailed information only for the PCI device at address 00:02.0:

00:02.0 VGA compatible controller: Intel Corporation 3rd Gen Core processor Graphics Controller (rev 09)

DeviceName: Onboard IGD

Subsystem: Dell Device 055e

Flags: bus master, fast devsel, latency 0, IRQ 42

Memory at f0000000 (64-bit, non-prefetchable) [size=16M]

I/O ports at f000 [size=64]

USB Devices

The lsusb command in Linux is used to list and display information about the USB (Universal Serial Bus) devices connected to the system. It provides detailed information about each connected USB device, including its vendor ID, product ID, and device description, which helps in identifying devices such as keyboards, mice, printers, storage devices, and other peripherals. By default, lsusb shows a concise list of devices, but it can be extended with options to display more detailed information. For example, lsusb -v provides verbose output, showing configuration details, device descriptors, and vendor/product IDs. This command is invaluable for troubleshooting hardware issues or identifying USB devices when setting up or maintaining a system.

Basic lsusb Command

List all connected USB devices:
lsusb

This command provides a concise output of all USB devices attached to the system:
Bus 002 Device 003: ID 8087:0020 Intel Corp. Integrated Rate Matching Hub
Bus 002 Device 002: ID 05e3:0610 Genesys Logic, Inc. USB 2.0 Hub
Bus 002 Device 004: ID 046d:c52b Logitech, Inc. Unifying Receiver
Bus 001 Device 005: ID 0781:5590 SanDisk Corp. Ultra USB 3.0

Verbose Output (-v)

Show detailed information about each USB device:
lsusb -v

This gives a more detailed description of the USB devices, including information about their configuration, vendor, and product IDs:
Bus 002 Device 004: ID 046d:c52b Logitech, Inc. Unifying Receiver
Device Descriptor:
bLength   18
bDescriptorType   1
bcdUSB   2.00
bDeviceClass   0 (Defined at Interface level)
bDeviceSubClass   0
bDeviceProtocol   0
bMaxPacketSize0   8
idVendor   0x046d Logitech, Inc.
idProduct   0xc52b Unifying Receiver
bcdDevice   00.01
iManufacturer   1 Logitech
iProduct   2 Unifying Receiver
iSerial   3 B8FFB8A0

Display Specific Bus/Device (-s)

Show information for a specific USB device by its bus and device number:
lsusb -s 002:004

This will display information only for the USB device at bus 002 and device 004:

Bus 002 Device 004: ID 046d:c52b Logitech, Inc. Unifying Receiver

Display USB Devices with Product/Manufacturer IDs (-d)

Show only devices from a specific manufacturer or product ID:
lsusb -d 046d:

This command filters and shows only devices from Logitech (with vendor ID 046d):
Bus 002 Device 004: ID 046d:c52b Logitech, Inc. Unifying Receiver

Monitoring Hardware

Monitoring hardware in a Linux system involves using specialized commands to track system health and performance. The sensors command, provided by the lm-sensors package, allows users to monitor hardware components such as CPU temperature, fan speeds, and voltage levels, helping to ensure that the system is operating within safe thermal limits. For example, running sensors will display the current temperature readings for various components:
sensors

Output might include details like:
coretemp-isa-0000

Adapter: ISA adapter
Core 0:   +35.0°C (high = +80.0°C, crit = +100.0°C)
Core 1:   +33.0°C (high = +80.0°C, crit = +100.0°C)

For a deeper dive into the system's hardware details, including memory, processor, and BIOS information, dmidecode can be used. This command provides a comprehensive dump of the system's DMI (Desktop Management Interface) table, revealing information such as motherboard manufacturer, processor type, and RAM capacity.

For instance:
sudo dmidecode -t memory

This command would return detailed information about the system's memory, such as:
Handle 0x0027, DMI type 17, 34 bytes
Memory Device
Array Handle: 0x0025
Error Information Handle: 0x0026
Total Width: 64 bits
Data Width: 64 bits
Size: 8 GB
Form Factor: DIMM
Type: DDR4
Speed: 2400 MHz

Together, these tools provide essential insights into the temperature and overall health of a system, as well as detailed information about the installed hardware components.

Checking Kernel Modules

Checking kernel modules in Linux is crucial for managing and troubleshooting system hardware and software components that require kernel-level support. The lsmod command lists all currently loaded kernel modules, providing a snapshot of which modules are active and their memory usage.

For example:
lsmod

This might display output like:
```
Module          Size  Used by
nvidia          20480000 30
snd_hda_intel     45056 3
```
If a specific module is missing or needs to be loaded, the modprobe command is used to load or unload kernel modules.

For instance, to load the vfat module for FAT filesystem support, you would use:
sudo modprobe vfat

Conversely, to remove a module, use:
sudo modprobe -r vfat
Additionally, dmesg is a powerful tool for viewing the kernel ring buffer, which contains diagnostic messages about the system's hardware, drivers, and modules. Running dmesg displays system logs that include messages related to kernel module loading, device initialization, and error reports.

For example:
dmesg | grep -i nvidia

This command filters kernel logs to display only entries related to the nvidia module, which is helpful for troubleshooting driver issues. Together, these commands help manage and monitor kernel modules, ensuring that the system operates smoothly and hardware components are supported.

Chapter 13: Managing Logs and Debugging

Managing logs and debugging are essential aspects of system administration in Linux, allowing administrators to monitor system behavior, diagnose issues, and ensure system stability. Logs provide a detailed history of system events, errors, and activities, and can be crucial for troubleshooting. The primary log files are located in the /var/log/ directory, and important files include syslog, dmesg, auth.log, and messages. Tools like journalctl provide access to systemd logs, offering a unified interface for querying logs across services.

For example, to view recent system logs:
journalctl -xe

This shows a detailed, real-time log output that can be filtered by date, priority, or service. For traditional logs, the cat, less, or tail commands are used to view the contents of specific log files.

For instance, to view the system message log, you might run:
tail -f /var/log/syslog

This shows the end of the log and updates in real time as new entries are added.

Debugging is another critical area that helps identify and resolve problems. Tools like strace and gdb allow for deeper inspection of running processes. strace is commonly used to trace system calls and signals of a running process, helping administrators to identify where a process might be failing.

For example:
strace -p <PID>

This traces the system calls of a process with the given Process ID (PID). On the other hand, gdb is used for more complex debugging, especially for programs written in C or C++, by allowing you to inspect memory, step through code, and evaluate expressions.

Together, log management and debugging tools enable administrators to gain insights into the system's operation, track errors, and resolve issues effectively, contributing to a more stable and secure environment.

System Log Files

On Debian-based systems, logging is centralized under the systemd journal, meaning that traditional log files like syslog, auth.log, and messages are not used in the same way as on other Linux distributions. Instead, journalctl provides access to all system logs, including kernel logs, service logs, and user-generated logs, stored in a binary format managed by the systemd-journald service. However, for compatibility, some traditional log files may still be present as symbolic links or may be used by certain applications.

Despite the shift to journal-based logging, key log files and their historical equivalents in Debian-based systems are still useful for administrators. These log files are typically located in the /var/log/ directory.

Here's a quick overview of their roles:

/var/log/syslog: Historically, this file captured general system messages, including boot processes, system errors, and application events. In the era of systemd, journalctl takes over this function, but the contents are often mirrored for compatibility.

/var/log/auth.log: This log file tracks authentication-related events, including user logins, sudo attempts, and other security-related messages. It's still maintained in systems that also utilize systemd logging, and can be accessed through journalctl using filters like journalctl -u sshd to view SSH-related logs.

/var/log/messages: Another log file that used to contain general system messages, like kernel and service messages. On modern systems, its functionality is often replaced by the system journal, and much of the information can be retrieved using journalctl commands.

To access logs via journalctl, users can run commands such as:

journalctl -xe   # View the most recent logs with details

journalctl -u sshd   # Filter logs related to the SSH service journalctl --since "2024-11-20" --until "2024-11-21" # View logs within a specific date range

With the shift to systemd, using journalctl is the preferred method for monitoring logs, and administrators should become familiar with its various filtering, search, and navigation options to manage logs effectively. While traditional files may still exist for some use cases, journalctl centralizes and simplifies log management, making it the primary tool for log access and system diagnostics on Debian systems.

Viewing Recent Logs

To view the most recent logs in the system journal, use the following command:
journalctl -xe
This command displays logs with more detailed information (-x provides explanations for certain messages) and continues to show logs until the user exits the view (-e for "end").

Viewing Logs for a Specific Service

If you want to view logs related to a specific service (e.g., SSH), use the -u option followed by the service name:
journalctl -u sshd

This shows logs for the SSH service. You can replace sshd with any other service name like apache2, nginx, etc.

Viewing Logs for a Specific Time Period

To view logs between two specific dates or times, you can use the --since and --until options:
journalctl --since "2024-11-20" --until "2024-11-21"
This command filters the logs to only show entries between November 20, 2024, and November 21, 2024.

Viewing Logs for a Specific Priority (e.g., Errors)

If you want to filter logs by priority, you can use the -p option. For instance, to view only error messages:
journalctl -p err
The priority levels can be emerg, alert, crit, err, warning, notice, info, and debug.

Following Logs in Real-Time

To view logs in real-time (similar to tail -f), use the -f option:
journalctl -f
This will continuously show new logs as they are written to the system journal.

Filtering Logs by Boot

To view logs from a specific boot session, you can use the -b option.

For instance, to view logs from the previous boot:

journalctl -b -1

The -1 option specifies the previous boot, and -0 would show logs from the current boot.

Searching for Specific Keywords in Logs

If you're interested in logs related to a specific keyword, you can use the grep command in combination with journalctl.

For example, to search for logs mentioning "failed":

journalctl | grep "failed"

This will filter through the logs and only display entries containing the word "failed."

Limit the Number of Logs

If you only want to view a limited number of recent logs, use the -n option followed by the number of entries you want to see:

journalctl -n 50

This command shows the last 50 log entries.

Viewing Logs

Viewing logs on Debian-based systems typically involves using journalctl, a tool that allows users to access logs stored in the systemd journal. The journal contains a wide variety of logs, including system messages, service logs, and kernel logs. With journalctl, users can filter logs by time, service, priority, and more. For example, the command journalctl -u sshd will display logs related to the SSH service, while journalctl -p err shows logs with error-level messages. You can also view real-time logs using journalctl -f or filter logs by specific dates with --since and --until. To limit the number of entries, -n can be used, such as journalctl -n 50 for the last 50 log entries. These commands provide a flexible and comprehensive way to monitor system activities and troubleshoot issues efficiently.

journalctl

journalctl is the primary command-line tool for viewing logs on systems that use systemd for initialization and service management, such as Debian-based distributions. It allows users to access a variety of logs, including system messages, service logs, kernel logs, and other diagnostic information stored in the systemd journal. With journalctl, users can filter logs by various parameters such as time, service, log priority, and boot session. For example, journalctl -u apache2 will show logs related to the Apache service, while journalctl -p err filters logs to only display error-level messages. It also supports real-time log monitoring with journalctl -f and the ability to view logs from specific time periods using the --since and --until options. This powerful tool offers detailed insights into system events and is essential for system administrators when diagnosing and troubleshooting issues.

View all logs

To view all logs stored in the systemd journal, use:
journalctl
This will display the entire system log in reverse chronological order.

View logs for a specific service

To view logs for a specific service, use the -u flag followed by the service name.
For example, to view logs for the ssh service:
journalctl -u ssh
Replace ssh with any other service name, such as apache2 or nginx.

View logs for a specific time period

To filter logs by date, you can use the --since and --until options.

For example, to view logs from November 1st, 2024:
journalctl --since "2024-11-01"

You can also use --until to specify the end date:
journalctl --since "2024-11-01" --until "2024-11-02"

View logs for the current boot session

To see logs from the current boot session, use the -b option:
journalctl -b

View logs from the previous boot

If you want to view logs from the previous boot session, you can use:
journalctl -b -1

Real-time log monitoring

To view logs in real-time (similar to tail -f), use the -f option:
journalctl -f
This will continuously display new log entries as they are written.

View logs by priority level

To view logs by priority, you can use the -p flag followed by the priority level.

For example, to view error-level messages:
journalctl -p err
Other priority levels include emerg, alert, crit, warning, notice, info, and debug.

View the last 50 log entries

To limit the number of log entries displayed, use the -n option.

For example, to view the last 50 log entries:
journalctl -n 50

Search for specific keywords in logs

To search for specific keywords in the logs, you can pipe the output to grep.

For example, to find logs related to "failed":
journalctl | grep "failed"

tail: Real-time monitoring of logs

The tail command is commonly used for real-time monitoring of log files on Linux systems, particularly with the -f option. When used with tail -f, it continuously displays the last few lines of a file and updates the output as new lines are added. This is especially useful for monitoring log files that are actively being written to, such as system logs or application logs. For example, to view the latest entries in a log file, you can run tail -f /var/log/syslog, and it will display new log entries as they are generated. This command is essential for system administrators and developers who need to troubleshoot issues, monitor system activities, or track specific events in real-time.

logrotate: Configuring log rotation

logrotate is a utility in Linux used to manage the rotation, compression, and deletion of log files to prevent them from growing too large and overwhelming the system. By configuring logrotate, system administrators can automate the process of rotating log files at regular intervals, keeping the system's storage organized and ensuring that old logs do not consume excessive disk space.

Configuration files, typically located in /etc/logrotate.conf or /etc/logrotate.d/, allow for fine-grained control over how logs are handled, such as how many old log files to keep, whether to compress old logs, and when to rotate them (e.g., daily, weekly, or monthly).

For example, a basic configuration might include keeping 4 weeks of logs, compressing logs after rotation, and triggering the rotation when the log file reaches a certain size. This helps maintain system performance, avoid running out of disk space, and ensure that logs are preserved for troubleshooting without unnecessarily bloating the filesystem.

Debugging System Issues

Debugging system issues in Linux involves a methodical approach to identify and resolve problems that affect system performance, functionality, or stability. Administrators often begin by checking log files, such as those in /var/log/, using tools like journalctl, dmesg, and tail to gather error messages or warnings that could provide clues. System resource usage can be monitored with commands like top, htop, or free to identify any processes consuming excessive CPU, memory, or disk space. Additionally, tools like strace and lsof allow for tracing system calls or identifying open files by processes, which can reveal hidden issues. In case of hardware-related problems, commands such as dmesg and lspci can be used to examine kernel messages and detect device errors. Through careful examination of logs, system metrics, and diagnostic tools, administrators can pinpoint the root causes of issues and apply appropriate fixes, ensuring the system operates smoothly.

Checking kernel messages for troubleshooting hardware issues

The dmesg command in Linux is a powerful tool for checking kernel messages and troubleshooting hardware issues. It displays the system's boot-up messages and logs generated by the kernel, which include information about device initialization, drivers, and hardware status. When hardware problems arise, such as issues with disk drives, network interfaces, or peripheral devices, running dmesg can reveal error messages, warnings, or other relevant data related to hardware malfunctions. For example, if a device is not being recognized or is having performance issues, dmesg can provide insights into whether the kernel is detecting the device correctly or encountering errors during initialization. The output can be filtered using tools like grep to focus on specific devices or errors, making it an essential command for diagnosing and resolving hardware-related problems in a Linux system.

View the entire kernel message buffer
dmesg
This will output all messages from the kernel, including hardware initialization logs and error messages.

Filter dmesg output for USB hardware
dmesg | grep -i usb

This will show messages related to USB devices, which is useful if you're troubleshooting issues with USB hardware.

Check for disk errors or storage-related issues

dmesg | grep -i sda

This filters the output to show only messages related to the sda device (typically the first hard drive), which can help identify disk-related issues.

View kernel messages since the system booted

dmesg -T

This adds a human-readable timestamp to the messages, making it easier to see when specific events occurred.

Check for specific error messages

dmesg | grep -i error

This filters the output to show only error messages, which can be useful for troubleshooting hardware problems.

Limit the output to recent messages

dmesg | tail -n 20

This shows the last 20 lines of the dmesg output, which can be helpful for seeing the most recent events, especially after a new device is connected or an error occurs.

Systemd Logs

journalctl -xe is a powerful command used in systems that utilize systemd to manage logs. It displays the most recent logs in an extended format, highlighting error messages, warnings, and critical system events. The -x option provides additional explanations for error messages when available, and the -e option ensures that the output scrolls to the end of the log, displaying the most recent entries. This makes journalctl -xe an invaluable tool for quickly diagnosing issues, particularly when a system is experiencing errors or failures. For example, if a service fails to start or a hardware issue arises, running journalctl -xe can provide detailed logs about the failure, such as service crashes, missing dependencies, or permission issues, helping administrators identify and resolve problems efficiently. It is commonly used in troubleshooting system failures, application crashes, and network-related issues.

View recent logs with extended data
journalctl -xe
This command shows the most recent logs with additional explanations for errors, warnings, and system events, making it easy to diagnose issues.

Filter logs by a specific service

journalctl -xe -u apache2

This shows logs related to the apache2 service, useful for troubleshooting web server issues.

View logs for a specific time frame

journalctl -xe --since "2024-11-01" --until "2024-11-22"

This command displays logs from November 1, 2024, to November 22, 2024, helping you narrow down logs to a specific period.

View logs for a specific priority level

journalctl -xe -p err

This shows only error messages (err priority), allowing you to focus on critical issues.

Show logs for the current boot

journalctl -xe -b

This filters logs to show only the entries from the current boot session, which is useful for diagnosing problems that occurred after a recent reboot.

Follow the logs in real-time

journalctl -xe -f

This option will display new log entries in real-time, making it helpful for monitoring ongoing issues or services that are actively logging errors.

Search for specific keywords

journalctl -xe | grep "failed"

This command filters the logs for entries containing the word "failed," which can help identify failed services or other issues quickly.

Using strace to trace system calls

strace is a powerful diagnostic tool used to trace system calls made by a program or process in Linux. When troubleshooting issues with a running application, strace -p <pid> allows you to attach to a process using its process ID (PID) and monitor the system calls it is making in real time. This can provide valuable insights into how the application interacts with the kernel, including file operations, network requests, memory allocations, and signal handling. For example, if a program is failing to open a file or connect to a network socket, strace can reveal the exact system call causing the issue, along with any error codes or failed attempts. By observing the sequence of system calls and responses, developers and system administrators can pinpoint performance bottlenecks, permission issues, and other bugs that might not be apparent from the program's output alone.

Trace system calls of a running process
strace -p <pid>
Replace <pid> with the process ID of the running application. This will trace and display the system calls made by that process in real-time.

Trace system calls of a program print output to file
strace -o output.txt <command>
This command runs the specified command (e.g., ls, curl, etc.) and saves all the traced system calls and their results into output.txt. This is useful for debugging and analyzing the system calls later.

Trace a specific type of system call
strace -e trace=open <command>
This command traces only open system calls (e.g., file open operations) for the specified command. You can replace open with other system calls such as read, write, connect, etc., depending on what you want to monitor.

Trace system calls with timestamps

strace -tt -p <pid>

The -tt option adds timestamps to each line of output, which can be helpful when tracking the sequence of system calls and correlating them with application behavior.

Trace system calls and filter by error codes

strace -e trace=error -p <pid>

This command will only show system calls that return errors, making it easier to identify what is failing in a process.

Trace a program and its child processes

strace -f <command>

The -f option allows strace to trace the system calls made by both the parent process and its child processes, which is useful for tracking how forked processes interact with the system.

Trace a program - limit number of system calls

strace -c -p <pid>

The -c option generates a summary of the system calls made by the process, providing a count and timing of each type of system call, useful for performance analysis.

Finding open files with lsof to diagnose issues

lsof (List Open Files) is a command-line utility in Linux that allows users to list all open files and the processes that have them open. This is particularly useful for diagnosing issues related to file access, resource leaks, or file system performance. For example, when a process is holding a file open and not releasing it, lsof can help identify which process is responsible, potentially leading to the resolution of deadlocks or resource contention. You can use lsof to find open files in a specific directory, check which processes are using a particular file, or even identify network connections. For instance, running lsof /path/to/file will show all processes currently accessing that file. Additionally, lsof -i can be used to list open network connections, while lsof -p <pid> will display all files opened by a specific process. By using lsof, system administrators can gain detailed insights into file usage and resolve a variety of system and application-related issues.

List all open files on the system
lsof
This command will list all open files across the system, including files, directories, and network connections that are currently being accessed by processes.

Find open files by a specific user
lsof -u username

Replace username with the name of the user you want to search for. This command lists all the files currently open by processes running under that user's account.

Find open files in a specific directory
lsof +D /path/to/directory
This will show all files that are open within a specific directory. Be careful, as this can take a long time for directories with many files.

List all open files for a specific process
lsof -p <pid>
Replace <pid> with the process ID of the application. This will show all the files that are currently open by that specific process.

List open network files
lsof -i
This shows all open network connections, including active Internet connections, and their associated processes.

Find which process is using a file
lsof /path/to/file

This will list the process (if any) that has the specified file open. It's useful when you need to know which program is locking a file.

List open files for a specific file extension
lsof *.log
This will display all open files with the .log extension. You can replace *.log with any file type or pattern to narrow down the search.

Show all open files and processes by port
lsof -i :<port_number>
Replace <port_number> with the port number you're interested in (e.g., 80 for HTTP). This shows which processes are listening on or have a connection to that port.

Check for deleted files that are still open
lsof | grep '(deleted)'
This is useful for identifying files that have been deleted but are still being held open by running processes, which can sometimes lead to disk space not being freed.

Appendices

Appendix A: Useful Linux Resources and Websites

Linux Documentation Project

Website: https://www.tldp.org

Description: The Linux Documentation Project is a vast collection of free resources for all things Linux, including guides, HOWTOs, FAQs, and manuals.

Linux Man Pages Online

Website: https://man7.org/linux/man-pages/

Description: The official online repository of man pages, which provide detailed documentation for Linux commands, system calls, and libraries.

ArchWiki

Website: https://wiki.archlinux.org

Description: ArchWiki is an extensive resource for users of Arch Linux, but it also serves as a helpful guide for users of all distributions with clear, in-depth documentation.

Ubuntu Documentation

Website: https://help.ubuntu.com

Description: Comprehensive documentation for Ubuntu users, including guides on installation, system administration, and troubleshooting.

LinuxQuestions.org

Website: https://www.linuxquestions.org

Description: A community-driven site for asking questions and getting answers related to Linux. A great resource for troubleshooting and problem-solving.

Stack Overflow

Website: https://stackoverflow.com

Description: A popular Q&A website where developers can get help on Linux programming issues, shell scripting, and much more.

The Linux Foundation

Website: https://www.linuxfoundation.org

Description: Provides training, certification, and resources for Linux professionals and enthusiasts. The site also hosts many important projects related to Linux development.

Red Hat Documentation

Website: https://access.redhat.com/documentation

Description: Detailed documentation for Red Hat Enterprise Linux, offering step-by-step guides and best practices.

Debian Wiki

Website: https://wiki.debian.org

Description: The Debian project's wiki offers extensive documentation about Debian installation, configuration, and management.

Linux Mint Forums

Website: https://forums.linuxmint.com

Description: The Linux Mint forums provide community-driven help and discussions on using the Linux Mint distribution.

GitHub

Website: https://github.com

Description: GitHub hosts many open-source Linux projects and is an excellent resource for learning, collaborating, and contributing to Linux-related software.

HowtoForge

Website: https://www.howtoforge.com

Description: Offers detailed tutorials and guides on setting up and managing Linux servers, systems, and software.

DigitalOcean Community Tutorials

Website:
https://www.digitalocean.com/community/tutorials

Description: A wealth of tutorials on various Linux topics ranging from basic system setup to more advanced topics like DevOps and cloud hosting.

SysAdmin Tutorials

Website: https://www.tecmint.com

Description: A site dedicated to Linux server administration, offering step-by-step tutorials on everything from network setup to security management.

Linux.com

Website: https://www.linux.com

Description: The official website for The Linux Foundation, featuring news, guides, and resources for Linux users and developers.

YouTube Channels for Linux Tutorials

Examples:

The Linux Foundation

Linux Academy

Description: Various channels dedicated to Linux tutorials, with video courses and practical demonstrations of Linux administration and development.

Linux Mint User Guide

Website: https://www.linuxmint.com/documentation.php

Description: The official Linux Mint user guide, a great resource for both new and experienced Linux users.

Linux Tutorials (by GeeksforGeeks)

Website: https://www.geeksforgeeks.org/linux-tutorials/

Description: A comprehensive set of tutorials covering a wide range of Linux topics, from beginner to advanced.

NixCraft

Website: https://www.cyberciti.biz

Description: A blog providing practical Linux and Unix administration tips and solutions to common problems.

Linode Documentation

Website: https://www.linode.com/docs

Description: A collection of tutorials and guides focused on cloud hosting and server management with Linux.

Appendix B: Troubleshooting Common Issues

Boot Issues:

Problem: The system doesn't boot, or you encounter a GRUB (bootloader) error.

Solution:

Use a live CD/USB to access the system.

Reinstall or repair GRUB using grub-install or boot-repair (for Ubuntu-based systems).

Check /etc/fstab for any issues with mounting drives.

Boot into rescue mode or use fsck to check and repair the filesystem.

Disk Space Issues:

Problem: System is running out of disk space, leading to performance issues or inability to install software.

Solution:

Use df -h to check disk usage and identify full partitions.

Remove unnecessary files with rm, find, or tools like bleachbit.

Clean package cache using apt-get clean (Debian-based) or yum clean all (Red Hat-based).

Move large files to an external drive or a different partition.

Networking Issues:

Problem: Network connection is down or intermittent.

Solution:

Use ping to check network connectivity.

Check network interfaces with ifconfig or ip a.

Restart the network service with systemctl restart network (CentOS/RHEL) or service networking restart (Debian/Ubuntu).

Check firewall settings with ufw status (Ubuntu) or firewalld (CentOS/RHEL).

Package Management Problems:

Problem: Issues with installing, updating, or removing packages.

Solution:

Ensure the system is up-to-date with apt update && apt upgrade (Debian/Ubuntu) or dnf update (Fedora).

Use dpkg --configure -a or apt-get install -f to fix broken packages on Debian/Ubuntu systems.

Clean the package manager cache with yum clean all (RHEL/CentOS) or dnf clean all (Fedora).

Remove or reinstall problematic packages using apt-get remove or yum remove.

Permission Issues:

Problem: Access denied or permission errors for files or directories.

Solution:

Check file permissions with ls -l.

Change file permissions using chmod and file ownership with chown.

Use sudo to execute commands as a superuser for privileged operations.

Ensure proper user and group configurations in /etc/passwd and /etc/group.

Service Failures:

Problem: Services or daemons fail to start or stop.

Solution:

Check the status of the service with systemctl status <service-name>.

View detailed logs using journalctl -u <service-name> to identify specific errors.

Restart the service with systemctl restart <service-name>.

Use systemctl enable <service-name> to ensure the service starts on boot.

X Server or GUI Problems:

Problem: Issues with starting the X server or graphical interface.

Solution:

Check logs in /var/log/Xorg.0.log for errors related to X.

Restart the display manager with systemctl restart gdm (GNOME), lightdm, or sddm (KDE).

Reconfigure the X server with dpkg-reconfigure xserver-xorg (Debian/Ubuntu) or Xorg -configure.

If you experience screen flickering, check drivers and display settings using xrandr.

Kernel Panics or Crashes:

Problem: The system crashes or kernel panics during boot or operation.

Solution:

Check kernel logs with journalctl -k or dmesg for clues to the cause.

Investigate hardware issues such as bad RAM or a failing disk by using memtest86 or smartctl.

Boot into a previous kernel version or recovery mode from the GRUB menu.

Ensure that the kernel is up-to-date using apt-get update && apt-get upgrade or yum update.

Sound Issues:

Problem: No sound or audio device not detected.

Solution:

Use alsamixer to check audio levels and mute settings.

Restart the sound service using systemctl restart alsa-utils.

Reinstall sound drivers with apt-get install --reinstall alsa-base pulseaudio (Debian/Ubuntu).

Ensure the correct output device is selected using pavucontrol (PulseAudio Volume Control).

Failed System Updates:

Problem: System update fails or partially completes.

Solution:

Run apt-get update or dnf update to refresh repositories.

Clear the package manager cache using apt-get clean or yum clean all.

Manually fix broken dependencies using apt-get install -f (Debian/Ubuntu) or dnf check (Fedora).

Check for errors in the logs with journalctl -xe for more specific failure information.

High CPU or Memory Usage:

Problem: System is slow or unresponsive due to high CPU or memory usage.

Solution:

Use top or htop to identify processes consuming excessive resources.

Kill unresponsive processes with kill <pid> or kill -9 <pid>.

Check memory usage with free -m or cat /proc/meminfo.

Investigate running services with systemctl to stop unnecessary services or daemons.

www.ingramcontent.com/pod-product-compliance
Lightning Source LLC
LaVergne TN
LVHW022337060326
832902LV00022B/4094